Be a Reporter

A Beginner's Handbook

HARRY GOLDHAR

Chestnut Publishing Group

National Library of Canada Cataloguing in Publication Data

Goldhar, Harry, 1934–
    Be a reporter: a beginner's handbook

ISBN 1-894601-03-3

1. Journalism—Authorship—Vocational guidance. 2. Journalism—
Editing—Vocational guidance. 3. Reporters and reporting—Vocational
guidance. I. Title.

PN4781.G64 2002   070.4'023   C2001-904008-3

Designer John Zehethofer
Typesetting by Laura Brady

Printed and bound in Canada

Published by Chestnut Publishing Group,
4005 Bayview Ave., Ste. 610,
Toronto, ON M2M 3Z9 Canada
Tel: 416-224-5824 Fax: 416-224-0595
www.chestnutpublishing.com

For R.S.G., U.K. and S.H.

Contents

Foreword

They are not the stars of the written word. They seldom get bylines. They labour, usually anonymously, in print, broadcast and Internet newsrooms.

They are the editors who can turn a reporter's convoluted prose into literature, who can help writers work out the beginning, the middle and the end of their stories; they are the lovers of the language who ignore burgeoning ulcers to meet daily deadlines, who convey the gist of a 1,000-word epic in a five-word headline, lay out pages to guide the reader's eye and then get hell the next day when a typo mysteriously appears in the story they have lovingly edited.

Harry Goldhar belongs to this group. In fact, I would say he is one of the best editors in this country.

When I became Features Editor at the Toronto Star, he and I and a group of dedicated writers and copy editors launched an Insight section that won plaudits from Time magazine as one of the best such sections on the continent. High praise indeed from a Luce publication.

Later, when I was assistant dean at the Graduate School of Journalism at the University of Western Ontario, Harry became an adjunct professor who visited the school regularly to teach the art of writing and editing. He was tough and demanding; the students groaned and moaned; then at the end of the academic term he ranked "tops" in the student ratings.

Harry went on to hire and teach numerous young journalists who joined the staff of the group of community papers he published in the metropolitan Toronto area.

This book, then, is a natural extension of his special talent, a gift, in portable form, to working journalists, to would-be journalists and communicators in general.

SHIRLEY SHARZER

Shirley Sharzer retired in 1993 as National Co-ordinator of Editorial Training and Development for the Southam Newspaper Group. Prior to that she held a number of senior editorial positions on Canadian newspapers, including deputy managing editor of the Globe and Mail. In 2000 she received the Order of Canada for her contributions to Canadian journalism.

Thanks

The mistakes are all mine. That's what you say at the end of a preface. It's done now, so let's get to the middle, to the thank yous to people who helped so much.

The first one goes to Stanley Starkman, who has spent more than 40 years in the publishing business in Canada and the U.S. He encouraged me from the beginning to write this book.

Second thanks goes to Shirley Sharzer, a trailblazer for women in journalism as she's been known for about 40 years. She went out of her way to get journalism professors to critique my early drafts.

Gerry Hall, John Miller, Nancy Burt, Dunc McMonagle, Don Gibb and Mel Tsuji, all journalists and teachers, made many good suggestions. Jim O'Leary and Stephen Kimber were generous with their time helping with the chapter on the Internet. John Lott and Pat Bell gave their time to read the manuscript and comment. Kenise Kilbride and Anne Carruthers corrected all my grammatical mistakes in the section on grammar.

David Potts, one of Canada's leading libel lawyers, made sure I wouldn't get you in trouble with the libel chapter.

All this brings us to the start of the preface:

This is a workbook and a beginner's text into a sometimes complicated, sometimes frustrating, an often fascinating and, yes, at times boring job that you have to learn by doing.

So turn the page and get going.

Some rules in journalism are meant to be broken, some you break only at your and other people's peril. You'll soon learn which is which, but don't be in a hurry to break the breakables. Learn the formula first.

Getting The Secret

A good newspaper is never nearly good enough but a lousy newspaper is a joy forever.

U.S. *author Garrison Keillor.*

There are two primary rules and one "secret" to writing a hard news story in a newspaper.

The rules:

- Get the five Ws up top.
- Organize the story properly.

The secret:

- Start with the right angle.

The five Ws are Who, What, Where, When and Why. Sometimes you add a How.

The right organization has the information decreasing in importance as you get further into the story.

The angle, simply, is the most interesting fact. Choose the right one and everything else should fall into place. That may sound simple. It isn't. I've called it a secret because it is the hardest thing for a beginning reporter to learn. In fact, many experienced reporters still have trouble with it. Don't be concerned if it takes a long time to get it right.

Now let's see how it works. Here are some facts to turn into a story.

Jeff Koen, who lives at 1823 College Avenue, took his wife to the doctor yesterday afternoon. They were expecting a baby next month and this was a regular visit for a check-up. On the way home, at about 4 o'clock, their jeep got a terrific broadside smash on the left side from a pick-up truck.

A terrific broadside smash.

Police said the accident happened at the corner of Dundas St. and Muriel Drive. The Koens were going west along Dundas, the truck coming south on Muriel. The driver of the truck was Karl Wyness, whose home is at 54 Apples Crt.

Mr. Koen was treated at Victoria Hospital for bruises. Two scalp cuts were stitched up and then he was released. His wife, Barbara, spent three hours in an operating room. She had a broken right leg, cuts and bruises, some chipped teeth and two cracked ribs. The hospital now lists her condition as satisfactory.

Doctors also performed a Caesarian section so she could deliver a seven-pound, three-ounce baby boy. The hospital says the baby's condition is good.

Police have charged Wyness with failing to stop at a traffic light and with drunk driving. He was obviously at fault.

That's the information. Let's go through how an experienced reporter thinks:

What's the angle, the most interesting thing? It's not the accident. That's one of many every day. It's not the police charges. They're common too. The most interesting thing is the most unusual one — a pregnant woman delivers a baby almost immediately after being injured in a car accident.

Now you have to write that while getting in the five Ws.

Using the angle we've chosen, the *Who* is Barbara Koen. *What* is the delivery of the premature baby. *Where* is in the hospital. *When* is yesterday. *Why* is the car accident.

Now you can write your lead (or lede as it's sometimes written to avoid confusion with the metal lead). The lead is the beginning of a story, the part that contains the five Ws and the angle. It's usually, though not always, one paragraph and short.

> A College Ave. woman delivered a premature baby in Victoria Hospital yesterday after suffering a broken leg and two cracked ribs in a car accident.

That's short and to the point. It's not literature (save that for a couple of weeks), but it does the job. You would probably have written it differently. That's OK. Give these same facts to five experienced reporters and you'll get five different leads, all properly written.

For example, here's another run at it:

> Barbara Koen spent three hours in the operating room yesterday, getting a broken leg and two cracked ribs repaired after a car accident — and delivering a seven-pound, three-ounce baby.

Writing The Story

Journalism is unreadable, and literature is unread.
Oscar Wilde.

Before writing the rest of the story, here are some guidelines:

- Always keep in mind the KISS principle: Keep It Simple, Stupid. Even if you have brains you can understand small words and simple sentence structures.
- Don't try to "write". Don't think "words". Think "ideas" and "facts". Your job is to get information to the reader. If you do that as simply and as quickly as you can, you will be "writing" in your own style.
- Don't repeat ideas. You'll bore the reader. A good writer will set up the story so that ideas flow naturally from each other. That's also something hard for a beginning writer to do.

Let's go back to the first lead we wrote.

> A College Ave. woman delivered a premature baby in Victoria Hospital yesterday after suffering a broken leg and two cracked ribs in a car accident.

That tells the whole story, doesn't it? Isn't there something wrong with starting with so much information that the reader doesn't have to continue?

The short answer is no. The lead is a synopsis and if the reader decides he's not interested in that kind of story and stops there, it's possible that you have still done your job well. Most people hurry through their newspaper. That creates a strong need to know quickly what the story is about. Long leads that never seem to get to the point can drive readers away, even if they are interested in the topic.

The prime purpose of a lead is to grab readers, to entice them to read on (even, you hope, if they're not interested in the topic). That's why the angle

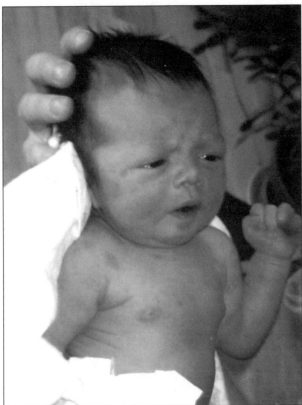

One baby, a broken leg and two cracked ribs.

Kim Abrahamse

goes up top. That's why you push the angle, the drama or whatever strength you have in the story to its legitimate limit in the lead. Stop short of bad taste and distortion but milk it for all it's worth.

Take a run yourself at some different leads for the story and you'll see how easy it is to distort.

Now let's write the rest of the story, starting with that first lead.

A College Ave. woman delivered a premature baby in Victoria Hospital yesterday after suffering a broken leg and two cracked ribs in a car accident.

Barbara Koen spent three hours in the operating room, doctors said, as they delivered the seven-pound, three-ounce boy by Caesarian section and took care of the other injuries.

Mrs. Koen was being driven home from a medical check-up by her husband, Jeff, when their car was hit at Dundas St. and

Muriel Dr. by a pick-up truck, police said. She was expecting next month.

Police charged the driver of the truck, Karl Wyness, 54 Apples Crt., with impaired driving and failing to stop at a red light.

The mother's condition is satisfactory, doctors said. Her husband was treated for scalp cuts and bruises and was released.

-30- (That's the traditional signal that a story has ended.)

Let's look at what happened.

- The most important idea, in my opinion (which may differ from your opinion and your editor's), was high in the story. As the story progressed the information became less important. As the basic ideas were written, the other details, like the names of the parents, were woven in. The judgement about the order of ideas should be based partly on what you think the readers would be asking themselves after each paragraph.

That construction will work only if you have the right lead (which means the right angle).

That organization is called the inverted pyramid, a catchy phrase whose definition doesn't really fit reality.

Theoretically, if you stack all the facts on lines that relate to their importance, with the most important on top, most facts will be on the top line with the other lines gradually getting shorter. That sets up a useful image. It also creates a story that readers can leave in the middle, just as they can leave a story after the lead, and it helps editors shorten stories by trimming from the bottom.

- Some of the information has been left out. You should use only what you need to get across the necessary ideas. You're not writing a book or the minutes of a meeting. And don't forget KISS.
- One of the facts left out was the "terrific broadside smash". That's an opinion, not a fact. If you can't quote someone saying that, leave it out. Don't take for granted everything you read or hear from official sources (or, especially, from other reporters). Even worse is the statement that Wyness was at fault. He's been charged only, not found guilty in court. If you suggest fault, in any way, you've committed libel.

- There's probably too much attribution in the story. There's little chance the police or hospital would be giving false information in this case, but this is an exercise so let's do it right. You're getting this information second hand. You don't know that it's true.
- There is no chronological order in the story. On rare occasions chronology works, but mostly you should consider it a deadly mistake for a simple news story.
- Be consistent. If you write Ave. you must write St., not Street. Look back at the facts of the story and you'll see both styles were given. You must study your newspaper's style guide.
- Cut, cut, cut words. If you think ideas, instead of words, you'll be surprised how many unnecessary words we all use. I trimmed several times to get the story above down to what it is. You may find even more ways to make it more concise.

For the exercise, let's examine the previous paragraph, which I purposely didn't try to trim: Is it really necessary to use "all" in "we all use"? How about the word "down" in "above down to. . ."? Is the word "above" necessary? Or "even" in "even more ways"? (And how about "really" in "really necessary" in this paragraph?) There are more ways to trim the previous paragraph. Look for them.

- Unfortunately, doing journalism means you have to think. Here's an example of why: The information in the story says the Koen car, travelling west, was hit on the left side by the truck travelling south. How come the truck, coming from the right side of the car, hit it on the left side? Which is the left side in this case: looking at it from the driver's point of view or while facing the front of the car? You need to ask.

It's Your Turn

In the old days men had the rack. Now they have the Press.
Oscar Wilde.

Here's another set of facts. Spend some time thinking about the angle and then write the lead.

At 386 Norwood Ave., at 3:45 p.m. this afternoon, John MacPherson, superintendent of the Almond Building, which is at that address, phoned the fire department to say a back room on the ground floor of the five-storey building was on fire. He was pretty excited, as you can imagine. He'd worked at that place for 43 years and nothing like it had ever happened before. He's 61 years old and he knew the building was old and mostly made of wood. It was a storehouse and retail sales centre for antique furniture, which is pretty flammable.

The firemen were at the scene in 10 minutes, they said, but they couldn't control the fire and the building was destroyed. It was all over by 9 p.m. It really lit up the sky in the evening.

Damage was estimated by the firemen and the owner of the business at $2.5 million, partly because of all the antiques, like Louis XIV chairs, early pioneer furniture and kitchen equipment. The owner, of both the building and the business, which was called London Antiques Ltd., is Peter Olaes. He said, "I've got lots of insurance, but that won't make up for the loss of all those old things, some of which it's impossible to replace. What a loss! It's terrible! And it's going to be horrible trying to start up the business again.

"But the worst thing is that my dog Pokey died in the fire. He came to work with me this morning and I guess in the confusion he got trapped. I don't know how the kids are going to take this."

Olaes has two daughters, Maria, who is five years old, and Eliza, who is seven years old. Pokey, a white American bulldog, was still a puppy and had been with the family for only three months, but had already won their hearts.

Fifteen people were evacuated from the building. No one, other than Pokey, was hurt.

"We're still trying to find out how the fire started," said Fire Chief Roger Alensonn.

Close the book now and write your lead, then come back to the book and turn the page.

Sharpening The Lead

Four hostile newspapers are more to be feared than a thousand bayonets.

Napoleon Bonaparte.

The angle is Pokey.

In my years of teaching journalism that angle caused the hottest discussions but left the most lasting impression after graduation.

Is the death of a dog of the same consequence as the loss of irreplaceable antiques, the dislocation in human affairs caused by a major fire and a $2.5 million loss? What kind of cheap journalism rates the death of an animal with so much importance? Those were the complaints of many students about Pokey being the angle.

In a story of this kind, no one cares what you think about the worth of a dog (even if you think it's the most important thing). This story is about Olaes and his disaster.

If Olaes thinks the loss of his dog is more upsetting than the loss of the antiques and the disruption in his business, that's the angle. It is the most interesting fact. It puts a twist on the story and to some people it would be surprising. And it sets you up for writing the rest of the story.

Pokey is what your lead should be about. For example: The loss in dollars yesterday was 2.5 million, but the bigger hurt to Peter Olaes was two broken hearts caused by the fiery death of a beloved white bulldog. (You should check that two hearts were in fact broken.)

Even if you got it right, it wouldn't have been easy to write. If you got it wrong, keep trying for one of your own leads. Expect it to take many tries.

Here's an example of how you might have to struggle. The following is a series of attempts by a journalism student, who was given minimal help, to produce a story from a fact sheet.

Pokey caused the hottest discussions.

FIRST ATTEMPT:

A young bridegroom was arrested yesterday after he and his seventeen-year-old bride drove away from the Shell service station at 277 Highbury Ave. without paying their gasoline bill.

Mark Daniel Panetta, 19, of Walled Lake, Manitoba, is charged under the Criminal Code with a theft of less than $200.00 value.

He appeared in court earlier today.

Panetta, who did not have enough money to cover the gasoline tab, spent the night at Police Headquarters.

His wife stayed at the Rotholme Women's Residence overnight.

The amount of the gasoline bill? Ten dollars.

-30-

SECOND ATTEMPT:

A man was arrested yesterday and charged with theft for not paying a $10 gasoline bill at the Shell station at 277 Highbury Ave.

Police say Mark Daniel Panetta, 19, of Walled Lake, Manitoba, did not have enough money with him to cover the tab.

Panetta, who was recently married, spent the night at Police Headquarters.

His bride stayed at the Rotholme Women's Residence.

Panetta appeared in court earlier today.

-30-

THIRD ATTEMPT:

A man on his honeymoon spent last night in the Podunk Police Headquarters after being charged with not paying a $10 gasoline bill.

Police say Mark Daniel Panetta, 19, of Walled Lake, Manitoba, did not have enough money with him to cover the tab.

Panetta's bride stayed at the Rotholme Women's Residence.

Panetta appeared in court earlier today.

-30-

FOURTH ATTEMPT:

A nineteen-year-old man on his honeymoon will spend a second night in a Podunk jail after being convicted of not paying a $10 gasoline bill at the Shell station at 277 Highbury Ave.

His seventeen-year-old wife stayed at the Rothome Women's Residence last night.

When arrested by police last night, Mark Daniel Panetta, 19, of Walled Lake, Manitoba, did not have enough money with him to pay the bill.

-30-

FIFTH ATTEMPT:

A man on his honeymoon spent last night in a Podunk jail after being charged with not paying a $10 gasoline bill.

Police say Mark Daniel Panetta, 19, of Walled Lake, Manitoba, did not have enough money to cover the tab.

Panetta's bride stayed at the Rotholme Women's Residence.

Panetta appeared in court earlier today, and was sentenced to one day in jail.

-30-

SIXTH ATTEMPT:

A nineteen-year-old tourist on his honeymoon will spend a second night in a Podunk jail after being convicted of not paying a $10 gasoline bill at the Shell station at 277 Highbury Ave.

His seventeen-year-old wife stayed at the Rotholme Women's Residence last night.

When arrested by police last night, Mark Daniel Panetta, 19, of Walled Lake, Manitoba, did not have enough money with him to pay the bill.

-30-

SEVENTH ATTEMPT:

A 19-year-old tourist in Podunk on his honeymoon will spend a second night in jail while his wife sleeps elsewhere.

Mark Daniel Panetta, 19, of Walled Lake, Manitoba, was convicted in court today for not paying a $10 gasoline bill at the Shell station at 277 Highbury Ave.

Panetta's 17-year-old wife stayed at the Rotholme Women's Residence last night.

Police say that when Panetta was arrested last evening, he did not have enough money with him to pay the bill.

-30-

By this time we were all sick of Panetta. We changed the last lead to say he would "spend a second night in jail alone because of an unpaid $10 bill" instead of "while his wife sleeps elsewhere", trimmed the story a bit and kissed it good night. None of the previous attempts got all the right information into the first sentence.

Now finish the Pokey story using the right angle in the lead. You should find that it almost writes itself; one thing should lead to another if you keep in mind the questions a reader would ask.

Here's an exercise for next month: Look for stories written in small papers where the reporters are not properly trained. See how often you find the angle in the last paragraph.

(Warning: New reporters often try *too* hard to make the lead exciting or different. If someone blows up Vancouver, don't look for another angle. If the general fact is the most interesting, that's the lead (Vancouver disappeared today, blown off the face of the earth. Winston Churchill is dead. The Toronto Maple Leafs have won the Stanley Cup.); *the angle is the most interesting part of the story.*

Getting All The Facts

You try to tell me anything about the newspaper business! Sir, I have been through it from Alpha to Omaha, and I tell you that the less a man knows the bigger the noise he makes and the higher the salary he commands.

Mark Twain.

Writing a story properly is only half a reporter's job, the lesser half. If you can't get the story and all the needed facts, there's nothing to write.

That means that even though you may be bored with the Koen story, we're going to have a quick look at it again. If you think about it you'll come up with lots of unanswered questions.

Why a Caesarian section? Did the accident induce the birth or did the doctors want to save Barbara Koen a month of inconvenience? Was the baby born first or the injuries taken care of first? Did the injuries make the birth more complicated? Was there danger of complications? Over seven pounds for a premature baby seems big — any comment from the doctors or parents? How come Jeff Koen was home at 4 p.m. to drive his wife? (Does that seem like a dumb question? Ask it. You will often be surprised at answers to questions like that.) What does Barbara Koen say about what happened? What about Jeff Koen's comments? Do the Koens have other kids? Any of them premature? Were either or both of the parents born prematurely? Has the hospital had similar occurrences? If the answer is yes, get as much information as you can. What about Wyness? History of accidents with strange results? Etc., etc. etc.

Those are all questions worth asking because the answers sometimes will be surprising.

There are three methods that will help you think of questions like those. The first works well. The second is iffy. The third is essential.

1. Imagine possible angles.

Jeff Koen was home because he was in a car accident the day before. Barbara Koen delivered three other babies following accidents. The hospital has had a run of strange emergencies. Both Koen parents were prematurely born following accidents. Wyness had been drinking to celebrate the fact his wife just had a baby, or he has killed several people in his car and is now making it up by bringing a new person into the world.

Don't be frightened by impossible ideas. Sometimes you can't make up anything as wild as the truth.

2. Ask the five Ws about everything.

The parents: If you ask *who* they are, you might find they are defensive driving instructors. If you ask *what* they are, that may raise questions about whether they have had other premature children. If you ask *when* you learn they had just visited their doctor. If you ask *why*, you'll wonder why you're doing this. The answer is that sometimes it works, if you have time. For example: Who is Wyness? Where was he going? Where was he drinking? Why was he drinking? Why was he at that corner? What was he drinking? What's his job? Imagine the possibilities.

3. Step back from the details of the story and look at the forest, not the trees.

Put the story into the context of the world around it and questions will start popping. For example, did everyone have insurance? How will the premature birth disrupt life for the Koens, especially with the mother injured? How will she look after a new baby?

When you can't think of any more questions, ask if there's anything that you have missed.

Asking *almost* all the right questions will become second nature eventually. But even then, you usually can't get them all answered the first day if you have a major story.

Here's an exercise. Make a list of questions for the following scenarios:
A fire: A private home owned by a family of five. A condominium townhouse in a cul-de-sac off a main street in Podunk.
A plane crash: A small executive jet carrying three people. It hit a hydro relay tower in a field outside Podunk during a heavy snowfall.
A retirement: The mayor, who rose from rags to riches, retires at age 87.

The mayor's frequent dinner guest.

IMSI

When he's reminiscing he mentions how his family used to let pet animals eat at the kitchen table. He even has an old photo to prove it.

Compare your list of questions with fellow students.

Here's another exercise: Look at breaking stories in your local newspaper. Think of unanswered questions. Check the paper the next couple of days to see if your questions would have turned up new angles. That's an important job for a reporter on a continuing story – finding those new angles.

Getting It Right

It is rarely that people criticize errors; it's only the truth that they ask us to retract.

Gerard Filion, former editor of Le Devoir.

The most important rule in journalism, the one you must never break: Be accurate.

It is too easy to make mistakes. An example:

Spell the other name for Coke, the soft drink.

Did you write Coca Cola?

Wrong. Look it up.

Always look it up.

Always ask the person you are interviewing to spell his or her name, then double check that you've got it right. Don't take anyone else's word for how to spell a name.

Try this test: Write from memory the full names of 10 of your friends. Now ask mutual friends to spell those friends' names. Now collect all the answers and check with your 10 friends to find out how many correct answers you have.

Here's a guideline to remember: Any reporter who does not spell correctly the name of the most famous hamburger joint in the world is not to be trusted. You would be surprised how many reporters get it wrong. They're too lazy to look it up, even though it is one of the easiest names to get wrong. Try it yourself from memory, then look it up. See how many times you have to check it over the next year because it is so easy to get wrong. It should be one of the words you write big and stick on the wall. Don't trust your memory.

Try this test: Ask 10 people who should be knowledgeable about Canadian history to spell the name of the first prime minister of the country. Try it yourself, then look it up, in an encyclopedia only. Too many other books or publications get it wrong.

In the Koen story, about the premature baby born after a car accident, did you consider that Jeff can also be spelled Geoff? A reporter should ask about that.

These past examples are simple ones. When your story gets complex, it gets easier to make major mistakes. You must try to think of all the possible ways you can get it wrong, including someone giving you false information or trying to trick you. It's also possible for you to misinterpret information that is correct, but not clear. Verify as often as you can.

Here are some true stories.

This is one of my favourite goofs:

The front page of the Toronto Star had a big spread in its first edition, during the Cold War days, reporting that the diplomatic community in a Far East nation was furious over a shipment of many boxes of unknown goods from an East European country to its embassy. The shipping crates were labelled with the outline of wine glasses and umbrellas. The reporter (an experienced, respected one) asked who could believe the embassy needed that many glasses and/or umbrellas shipped from the homeland. What was really in the boxes? The story disappeared before the end of that day's run. Wine glasses are an international shipping symbol for fragile contents. Umbrellas mean don't get the contents wet.

Here are some favourite goofs from other journalists, all of which contain a lesson to be learned.

• Another Toronto-based newspaper, the Globe and Mail, once ran a headline that said two people in Prince Edward Island had been convicted of a major crime. The copy editor who wrote the headline goofed badly — the reporter had written that the two had been charged, not convicted.

Clark Davey, managing editor at the time, recalls the mistake was caught in time, sort of. The presses had to be stopped and 60,000 copies of the first edition burned.

• Senator Richard (Dic) Doyle recalls in his book *Hurly-Burly* another incident at the Globe that happened when he was editor-in-chief.

A Montreal bureau reporter, writing about political intrusions on the judicial process, named, among others, Treasury Board president Jean Chretien (later prime minister). Chretien complained that the only information he had sought from a judge was the time when a case might come to court.

The reporter had taken the words he used from a letter a judge had written to the justice minister, a safe enough source one would expect. The Globe had decided, said Doyle about the wording, that the public interest "demanded its ventilation".

Chretien sued. On the advice of its lawyer, the Globe settled for $5,000.

A long time later, Doyle wrote, he met Chretien at a Rideau Hall dinner party. Chretien beckoned Doyle over to meet Mme Chretien and announced, "This is the man who paid for your piano! I think of him every time it is played."

• David Smyth, at the time a World Services editor of Associated Press in New York:

"Years ago the AP ran a South American news wire out of NY that included items in English of interest to the British West Indies and news in Spanish for Latin American newspapers.

"Some time in 1963 an item came in from a Santo Domingo correspondent saying that President Juan Bosch of the Dominican Republic had fired four army chaplains because he didn't like the political slant of their sermons to the troops.

"Since the news seemed of purely Caribbean interest the editor in NY sent it out in English only for the English-speaking islands.

"Some days later a furious protest came in from the Dominican government complaining that the AP was inventing sensationalist inflammatory and defamatory news items about the Bosch government.

"It turned out that an editor in a Mexico City daily had seen the item in English and thought it was of interest to his readers. So he had one of his staff translate it into Spanish in-house.

"The translator wasn't too good at his job and 'President Bosch Fires Four Army Chaplains' came out 'President Bosch Has Four Army Chaplains Shot By Firing Squad.'

"AP editors had a standing order from then on to use the word dismissed instead of fired."

• English-born Bob Cox was once editor of the Buenos Aires Herald. He recalls, "My own worst blooper was to put a headline on the news story about the birth of the Kennedys' son: Another John for the White House, me not knowing the U.S. meaning of john."

There are endless and surprising ways to make mistakes, as you have

Harry Truman shows off the big goof.   *Harry S. Truman Library*

probably already started to find out. To try to avoid them, never take anything for granted. Apropos to that thought is a funny sign that was popular
years ago: THIMK. 'Nnff said.

Also keep in mind the warning that became the rule of thumb at the City
News Bureau in Chicago, attributed to Arnold Dornfield: "If your mother
says she loves you, check it out." It is ironic that what used to be the most
famous newspaper goof in North America came out of the same city. In
1948, only hours after the polls closed for the U.S. presidential election on
Nov. 2, the re-elected president, Harry Truman, held aloft an early edition
of the Chicago Tribune for news photographers. The large banner headline
declared DEWEY DEFEATS TRUMAN. (This was different than the
mixed declarations following the first election of George W. Bush. In the
Truman election the Tribune was so sure of the winner it didn't wait for the
results. If it had, the early edition would have been late. In the Bush election the results were unclear for weeks.)

Go back to the paragraph at the beginning of this chapter about
McDonald's (yes, that's the right spelling). Did you find it hard to read?
There was a reason. Figure it out and then edit to correct the problem. And
by the way, the other name for Coke is Coca-Cola, with a hyphen.

The Right Lead

The way I had it is all gone now. The bars are gone, the drinkers, gone. There remain the smartest, healthiest newspeople in the history of the business. And they are so boring that they kill the business right in front of you.

New York newspaper columnist
Jimmy Breslin.

Sometimes it takes longer to get started than to write the whole story.

Your groping mind is telling you that you don't fully understand the story. Therefore, you don't have the right angle.

Here's a trick that could help: Put your notes away and pretend you're telling a friend or your mother over the phone what the story is about. That will make you stop thinking about a lead. It will force a quick summary and will often produce the right angle because your mind will push to the front the most interesting facts.

What would have happened with the Koen and Pokey stories?

"There's this pregnant lady who had a premature baby right after getting into a car accident."

"Some guy just lost his business and two and a half million bucks in a fire and he cares more about his dog dying."

Sometimes you don't understand the story because you don't have enough information. That is especially true in a story more complicated than one usually found in a police report. Sometimes you can't find a lead because there isn't a story there. Sometimes, of course, you can't find a lead because you're just being thick. Talk to your editor or another reporter you trust, but don't talk the whole story out. You may lose the spontaneity that makes the story flow.

If you have enough information, take some time to think about the story. You should have an idea of how it will all turn out.

Once you have figured out the point of it all, you must choose an approach. You can find lists, especially in journalism schools, of different types of leads, such as first person leads, anecdotal leads, descriptive leads, etc. They provide examples of different approaches, but you can do the same thing by having some fun, which is better than trying to categorize under labels. Besides, you shouldn't be thinking in categories. Let your mind loose.

Here's an exercise that should illustrate the many possibilities for writing leads:

Forty-five students were charged with being drunk and disorderly yesterday after a police raid at a get-acquainted party at the School of Journalism in Podunk University.

. . .

I was arrested for being drunk and disorderly yesterday, but when I appear in court next week I'll put the blame on the professors in the School of Journalism at Podunk University.

. . .

How would you plead in court if the police charged you with being drunk and disorderly after you innocently accepted an invitation to a get-acquainted party at your new school?

. . .

The professors were hiding under the tables and all us students were throwing cheese sandwiches at each other yesterday when police raided the School of Journalism at Podunk University.

. . .

Forty-five students lunched on bread and water today and can look forward to more of the same tonight in their prison cells, only 24 hours after a wild party at the School of Journalism at Podunk University.

. . .

The room smelled of alcohol and cheese and the noise of screaming students almost drowned out the policemen's whistles yesterday in a Podunk University classroom that now looks like a scene in a war movie.

. . .

Twenty broken whisky bottles, 11 violently ill professors, one destroyed classroom and 45 hungover students charged with being drunk and disorderly — that's what was left today after a police raid yesterday on the School of Journalism at Podunk University.

. . .

"I was having the time of my life and figured I couldn't have chosen a better school — then I suddenly found myself puking all over a cop," said one of the 45 journalism students charged yesterday with being drunk and disorderly at Podunk University.

. . .

In all the noise around him he heard a quiet moan. He turned his head and, just as he was hit in the nose by a sun-dried tomato sandwich, a police officer grabbed him.

. . .

Journalism professors at Podunk University, who have earned a reputation for throwing great parties to welcome new students, may have gone too far yesterday.

. . .

Bill Jones had been on the wagon for three months, but it was getting harder and harder. Yesterday, he fell off. It's not hard to blame him — his dog Pokey died a week ago, his wife ran off with his father three days ago, and yesterday he helped 45 new students to such a rousing welcome at the School of Journalism in Podunk University that they all landed in jail.

. . .

By 3 p.m. the party at the School of Journalism had become a brawl. The professors were hiding under the tables, the new students were throwing avocado pears and tomatoes at each other and wrecking their classroom. By 5 p.m., after a police raid at Podunk University, the 45 students were a lot quieter and sober — they were all in jail charged with being drunk and disorderly.

. . .

That was one wild party at staid old Podunk University yesterday.

. . .

Worth noting:

All the leads would probably drag the reader further, even if they don't all contain the same number of details. What they have in common is information about the specific event. None could be used for another story.

Some of these leads, which do not contain enough information, should be followed quickly by a paragraph or two with all the five W details.

Some leads are short, some long. Short leads are good. Sometimes long leads are better. Don't be a slave to an artificial limit like 25 or 35 words.

Some newspapers like you to get the angle or the kernel of the story into the first 10 words. Don't let that rule destroy a better lead.

Sometimes, if the story is short enough and you write well enough, you may want to build up to a surprise ending.

Once you've written a lead that makes you happy, put yourself in the reader's head. Would you ask *So what*? If so, rewrite.

Some reporters find it easier to get a focus for the story and then write it all before coming back to tackle a lead.

When you read newspapers and magazines pay attention to the leads that grab you and figure out why. Notice how newspapers differ; some like short and snappy leads, some take their time getting to the point, some don't mind leads that are a little complicated. The difference is often related to the type of reader. Racy tabloids expect to be read quickly on public transportation. Some newspapers are after more relaxed readers.

If you're having trouble organizing the story, it sometimes helps to put your notes aside and plough through writing most of it before going back to check details.

Here are some facts so you can try writing different leads. Have some fun, then follow each lead with the story so you see how different leads change the construction. (The details were taken by former University of Western Ontario journalism professor Mack Laing from a story that appeared in the Bangkok Post and keeps cropping up on the internet.)

> The pianist in this story is Myron Kropp. He is a U.S. concert pianist. He recently gave a concert in Bangkok. Bangkok has a very humid climate that makes it difficult to keep pianos in tune.
>
> The concert was in the music room of the Erawan Hotel. The ushers, who appeared to be recruits from the hotel dining room, had difficulty in getting the audience into the proper seats. There were a number of people who arrived late for the concert.
>
> Mr. Kropp entered from the right of the concert stage. He was wearing the usual black formal evening wear with a small white poppy in the lapel. He had sparse, sandy hair and a sallow complexion and appeared very slight. The pianist is best known for his interpretations of Johann Sebastian Bach.
>
> The piano he was to use was an ancient Baldwin concert grand. These pianos are known to require careful attention to keep them in tune, and this is difficult even with a new one, in a non-humid climate.
>
> It came with a round, screw-type piano stool. Concert pianists usually prefer a bench because they find that the swivel stools tend to do just that during violent passages of music. Mr. Kropp

left the stage briefly, apparently to inquire about a bench. There wasn't one.

Humid weather causes the felt material used to separate the black and white keys on a piano to swell. This leads to sticking keys. The key, one of them, that stuck this time, was the D in the second octave.

Mr. Kropp had included in his program the D-Minor Toccata and Fugue, which has a difficult "raging storm" passage. He got through this, but appeared to be losing patience in a later work (the Prelude and Fugue in D-Major) in which the second-octave D plays a major role.

Some of the audience later questioned whether the sticky keys justified the language they claimed they heard Mr. Kropp using. One member of the audience sent his children out of the room.

At another point in the program, the piano stool suddenly swivelled, and the pianist found himself, in full swearing form, facing the audience directly. Someone in the audience started to laugh, and chuckles swept the hall.

Kropp went back to the keyboard, left the fugue unfinished, and started into the Fantasia and Fugue in G-Minor. The G key in the third octave started to stick. The pianist started to use his foot, kicking the piano in an apparent effort to make it behave. But instead, the front leg of the piano bent inward. This left the piano with about a 35-degree list from the level. The audience gasped, sensing that if the piano fell, the pianist would lose, at least, several toes.

Mr. Kropp got up from the piano and slowly left the stage. Some thought he was finished, and began to applaud. He reappeared, armed with the red-handled fire axe from backstage.

The reviewer says he thought, when the pianist began chopping at the piano legs, that he was just trying to get it level again. But he kept on even after the left leg of the instrument was shattered. The ushers, apparently, heard the sound of chopping and of snapping piano wires, and rushed in and finally managed to drag the angry pianist from the stage.

Murder, You Write

Printed in the sage brush country of the Lillooet every Thursday, God willing. Guarantees a chuckle every week and a belly laugh once a month, or your money back. Subscription: $5 in Canada. Furriners: $6. This week's circulation 1769, and every bloody one of them paid for.

Editorial Page, Bridge River-Lillooet News, published in the 1950s by Ma Murray.

The more you write, the easier it gets. Turning the following facts into stories may seem like a chore, but like your mother used to say, it's good for you.

Much of the information, but not all, comes from real situations. Wherever possible, check to make sure everything you write is true and correct. Take time to think about the angle. What would be of most interest to a reader?

MURDER

Bradley Kinston works as a financial advisor at Intercorp Funds Inc. in downtown Podunk. Yesterday he tried all afternoon to call his wife, Kaiko, at home because he wanted to warn her he was bringing home a visiting fireman for dinner and he knew she was planning to run their two daughters to ballet classes late in the afternoon. He wasn't worried about not being able to reach her but he thought it best to take the visitor, Owen Learner, to a restaurant for dinner instead.

He arranged to meet Learner, from the company's head office in Bigbopper, at 6 p.m. at the High Road Restaurant downtown at Charles St. and Summit Ave. At 5 he drove home just to check on what was happening.

This is what he told police happened next:

When he got to his two-storey, three-bedroom home on Laurel Rd., in the west end of Podunk beside the Slower River, he found the front door unlocked. He stepped inside and called his wife's name several times, but there was no answer. He tried calling his daughters' names too, Kate and Mary, but didn't expect an answer because they were supposed to be at

She didn't answer.

IMSI

their ballet classes. He thought, too, that if they were home they would have called out when he called his wife's name.

He went into the kitchen to see if anyone had left him a note. Nothing. He did notice that there were some dirty dishes on the kitchen table, something his wife seldom left out. She was a stickler for tidiness. In fact, she often scolded him for being too sloppy, like leaving newspapers on the living room coffee table or not putting his CDs away. He noticed an open bottle of milk, some drinking glasses and a half-finished loaf of cinnamon bread, among other things.

He wondered about the untidiness, but wasn't especially disturbed — until he started to leave and looked towards the little office beside the dining room that his wife used to run her small modelling business. She had been a successful model herself, but the business had been going slowly the last few months.

He saw his wife lying on her left side in the doorway, in only her underwear, with blood on the floor around her. She wasn't moving.

He rushed over to her and was stunned. She wasn't breathing and her throat had been cut open. There were also deep wounds in her chest and abdomen.

He didn't know what to do. What he saw didn't seem real. For a few seconds he couldn't move. He thought of mouth to mouth resuscitation but realized the problem was the loss of blood and what appeared to be knife wounds. He couldn't think of what he could do to try to help. Then he thought of calling for an ambulance. Was there something he could do before calling for help? All that thinking took only seconds, yet he thought he was wasting precious time and panicked. He rushed to the phone and couldn't remember the emergency number. . . 999? 119? He stopped, took a deep breath, and dialed 911. Then he panicked again.

He couldn't remember later what he told the operator. "Help, help," he thought he had said at some point, and that he had repeated the word blood several times. It seemed to take forever to tell them what had happened.

Later police said the call came in at 5:18 p.m. yesterday and an ambulance was at the house by 5:24 p.m. A police car arrived at 5:27 p.m.

Kinston was in shock, police told a press conference at the Podunk police headquarters this morning.

Insp. Kenneth Grayson, in charge of the investigation, said that Mrs. Kinston had been using her computer, which was still logged on to the Internet when police arrived.

He said police immediately retrieved information from the computer, which they put on a disk, but he refused to tell anything about the information.

He did say that they filed a request with Mrs. Kinston's service provider, Baycrest OnLine, for access to all her e-mail and the screen names she used. They asked for the same information for her husband.

In answer to questions, Grayson said it was possible that Mrs. Kinston knew her killer or killers and let them enter the house. He said no strange fingerprints were found. There was no weapon found. The wounds appeared to have been made by a long knife, he said, but he couldn't say for certain.

Police were still studying evidence, he said.

He described Mrs. Kinston as 5 feet 9 inches tall, 135 pounds, 37 years old and with long black hair.

Grayson said that after an investigation they were satisfied that Bradley Kinston was at work when his wife was killed. They put the time of death at between 1:30 and 3:30 yesterday afternoon.

Grayson refused to say whether anything had been stolen or disturbed in the house.

He said the Kinston daughters had been taken to their ballet class by the mother of a friend, who had left word at their school that she was taking Kate and Mary.

Write the story as if your newspaper will be published that afternoon.

Make a list of questions you would ask the police later. Make a list of other people you would speak to and then list the questions you would ask them.

Compare your lists with your fellow students'.

Write a solution to the crime in the form of a news story about the person who has been charged with murder.

DOCTORS

The very large Hotel Hermitage, with 340 rooms in the west-end of Podunk, hosted medical specialists from all over Silver County who assembled there Friday, Saturday and Sunday for the first annual Silver Conference on Diabetes.

They took over the whole hotel and other travellers who wanted to stay there for the weekend had to be turned away. Some were sent to the nearby Hotel Wilson, which also filled quickly. Some travellers could not find rooms in Podunk and had to travel miles to find a motel or hotel.

The spouses and children of the doctors toured the Saltmine Copper Refinery Saturday morning and then had the afternoon free for shopping after a lavish lunch at the hotel. On Sunday there was a soccer game between families of West Silver and East Silver, won by East Silver 2-1.

There were 28 seminars, most dealing with advances in the treatment of diabetes mellitus, or sugar diabetes, caused by a lack of insulin.

Insulin is used by the body to carry glucose from the blood stream across cell walls so the body can get nourishment. When there isn't enough insulin produced, the glucose stays in the blood and is secreted from the body in urine. When that happens the kidneys draw water from the rest of the body to create enough urine. In the old days, when doctors wanted to test for diabetes mellitus, they tasted the urine. If it was sweet, the patient had diabetes mellitus, which is different from diabetes insipidus.

Diabetes insipidus is the result of a lack of vasopressin, which helps the kidneys concentrate the urine to conserve water while excreting body wastes. When the kidneys can't concentrate the urine they produce a lot of dilute urine. To do that, the kidneys draw water from the rest of the body, as also happens in diabetes mellitus. In diabetes insipidus the taste of the urine is not sweet, but "tasteless," which is what insipidus means.

In both forms of diabetes the victim is very thirsty and urinates a lot.

"We had some really exciting seminars and there were some fascinating sessions dealing with new developments," said Dr. James Woodvimmer, secretary of the Conference.

Most victims of diabetes mellitus inject themselves with insulin regularly. Recently there have been developments with pumps that secrete insulin through the skin. In the last year researchers in Indonesia have been working on a time-release capsule that will dissolve in the stomach over a three-year period, releasing a measured amount of insulin.

At the current stage, said Dr. Joshi Suskama, a diabetes expert invited as special guest to the Conference, the capsule can be used only after the correct dosage is established, which can take months. There could also be a problem if the need for a change in dosage occurs. That could be solved by changing the life expectancy of the capsule, he said, for example from three years to three months or any other time period. At present, that's a stage that still hasn't been developed.

But even the three-year dosage is an "advancement in technique that will make life easier for millions of people," said Dr. Woodvimmer.

Dr. Suskama, who was born in nearby Willowby of an Indonesian father and Irish mother, both medical missionaries, has been doing research in Indonesia for the past 14 years. His brother and his first child died of diabetes mellitus.

"I'm driven to do this research," he said to loud and long applause at his keynote speech Saturday.

"If we had the capsule I'm developing 15 years ago my brother and son would still be here. They had such severe cases and so suddenly that doctors could not cope fast enough."

He said he returns to Willowby once a year to attend special remembrance ceremonies, the only time he takes a holiday because he works relentlessly trying to save other people from dying of diabetes. He combined this year's trip with the Conference.

He said he would be happy to return next year when, he hoped, he'd be able to announce the creation of a capsule that is self-regulating, that is, it would release insulin according to readings it would take itself from the patient's blood.

"He's more than welcome," said Dr. Woodvimmer. "At one point the delegates rose to their feet and applauded for two minutes. Without a doubt, he was the highlight of the Conference."

But Dr. Woodvimmer's daughter, Astrid, 10, wasn't as happy. During the soccer game she broke her leg in a tangle of players.

"What a dumb bunch of doctors," she said. "None of them at the game knew what to do about a broken leg."

PUPPIES

Podunk police issued a press release today saying they would be increasing their foot patrol activity by 40 per cent in the Bayview Bridges area starting tomorrow.

Instead of five officers at all times on the streets during three shifts, there will now be eight policemen from 8 a.m. to midnight on two shifts.

At the same time, police announced they would increase investigations into rumours that there have been pitbull fights in the area.

Police Sgt. Albert Wellsprig, the force's public relations officer, said police visited three locations over the past month where concerned citizens said there were dog fights.

The citizens, all residents of the area, said they were sometimes disturbed at night by rowdiness and barking.

"As yet, officers have found nothing wrong taking place," he said.

He said one visit was to the home of a man who owns nine unregistered dogs, all of various breeds, but he said he was a breeder and police could find nothing wrong.

Sgt. Wellsprig said the rumours of dogfights might have been started by the reaction in the community to the fact that 13 pitbull puppies had been stolen or disappeared from the area in the past two months.

Yesterday a four-month-old pitbull was stolen from a 74-year-old man who was walking the dog on a leash on Bayview St. near Oakham Ave. He was stopped by four men who leaped out of a car in front of him and threatened him with knives if he didn't turn the dog over to them. The man said he was afraid for his safety, so he released his hold on the leash and the four men took the dog, led it into their car and drove off.

The day before one pitbull puppy was reported missing and another stolen. One had been fenced into a back yard on Lassiter Ave. In the other incident, a 12-year-old girl said she was walking her puppy on Bayview St. near John St., only three blocks from Oakham Ave., when two men grabbed the dog and ran off with it.

Police said pitbulls are prepared for illegal fights by trainers with methods that include making them tread water for long periods, making them run behind bikes for long periods and then increasing the speed by tying them to the backs of cars, feeding them high-protein food and training them to be aggressive. The dogs are also fed chemical supplements to slow bleeding, making them more durable in fights.

Sgt. Wellsprig said, "The puppy thieves are becoming bolder each time. The trouble started a couple of months ago with reports of missing dogs, but now we're getting puppy snatching in broad daylight."

Peter Enogh, owner of the Bark and Meow Pet Shoppe on Bayview St., who specializes in rare breeds and has sold most of the pitbull puppies in the area, says pitbull puppies are very friendly when they are young but are easy to train to be aggressive. Some grown pitbulls have been known to attack humans, he said, and can easily kill them, especially young children.

Let's see how careful you are. In your story about the pitbulls, did you check to make sure the figures were correct, or made sense, for how many police officers would be on different shifts? What did you do about it? Always check figures.

Tighten Up

A petty reason perhaps why novelists more and more try to keep a distance from journalists is that novelists are trying to write the truth and journalists are trying to write fiction.
British novelist Graham Greene.

Writing tightly is more than trimming unnecessary words. It means, as mentioned, not repeating ideas, which is hard to do. Getting the right lead helps.

Here are two examples, real ones, of the kind of stories reporters with little experience write. They needed tightening and fixing, which I've done to give you examples. The names and places have been changed. They are followed by stories for you to rewrite.

FIRST EXAMPLE:

A 25-year-old Alberta man has been found guilty of beating up a 56-year-old Parkinson's disease sufferer.

District court Judge Alan Campbell said Monday that after hearing all the evidence he believes the victim, Martin Wilson, and not the defendant, Thomas Embrose.

"I do not accept his evidence," said Campbell, adding that on the stand, Wilson's hands shook – an obvious symptom of his disease.

"Several parts of Embrose's answers did not ring true," said Campbell.

After reading out a summary of events from each witness's testimony, Campbell said Wilson's evidence, when compared to RCMP and medical reports, was more consistent, detailed and accurate than Embrose's.

Embrose and Wilson's daughter were in a common-law relationship at the time of the incident.

Campbell said that during the early-morning hours of June 28, 1997, Embrose and his wife drove to Anaheim, where Wilson was housesitting and taking care of his daughter's young son.

Embrose and his wife had been in Conradville for three days, and Wilson was upset that the couple left him with the child to go off drinking.

While Embrose said they had driven home to see his wife's son, Campbell said he was more apt to believe they had driven home to collect her bank card. He added that it was introduced in court that the couple was angry because Wilson had refused a request to send the card to Conradville a few days earlier.

A fight between daughter and father started at the front door and ended with Wilson falling down 10 to 12 steps and Embrose hitting him with pieces of wood and a thermos.

A nurse's report said Wilson had been "beaten up badly," and had bruises on his face, hands and knees. He had also suffered from a dislocated shoulder.

Embrose was also found guilty of smashing the windows in Wilson's car.

Sentence will be announced on March 20.

-30-

Here's a possible rewrite:

A 25-year-old Alberta man has been found guilty of beating up a 56-year-old man who suffers from Parkinson's disease, the father of his common-law wife.

District Court Judge Alan Campbell said Monday he noted that the hands of the victim, Martin Wilson, shook from the disease while he testified. Campbell said he did not believe the testimony of the defendant, Thomas Embrose, who denied hitting the older man. "Several parts of Embrose's answers did not ring true," said Campbell.

Campbell said he was more apt to believe Wilson that his daughter and Embrose had returned home from Anaheim to Conradville early June 28 last year to get her bank card, not to see her son.

Wilson was upset that the couple had left him with the child to go drinking after visiting him for three days, Campbell said.

Court was told the couple were angry because Wilson had refused to send the card to Conradville.

During an argument between daughter and father at the front door, Wilson fell down 10 to 12 steps. Campbell said he believed that Embrose hit Wilson with pieces of wood and a thermos.

He said Wilson's evidence, when compared to RCMP and medical reports, was more consistent, detailed and accurate.

A nurse's report said Wilson had been "beaten up badly" and had bruises on his face, hands and knees. He also suffered a dislocated shoulder.

Embrose was also found guilty of smashing the windows in Wilson's car.

The sentence will be announced on March 20.

-30-

An unanswered question: What were the charges? Beating someone up and smashing a window are not legal charges. If you read those stories carefully you should have noted that the rewrite adds that Embrose denied hitting Wilson. It would be easy to assume that without asking the reporter. Don't. That clause should not be there. Never assume. Despite repeating an idea, I'll repeat: Never assume. In fact, NEVER ASSUME! It is impossible to over-stress that idea.

SECOND EXAMPLE:

More than 50 women and children showed up on the streets of Podunk last night to protest their lack of control over their safety and their streets.

During the annual Take Back the Night rally, Podunk residents chanted, sang and protested the violence and fear that have prevented women from feeling comfortable in their own city.

"It is about our freedom from violence. That is our basic right," Karen Sinisalo, a coordinator with the Elizabeth Walmer Women's Centre, said today.

The march has been an annual event in Podunk since 1992.

Part of the protest was a discussion afterward at the United Church concerning where women feel unsafe.

Day or night, the bush trails many use to jog, ride their bikes or walk are never safe, said Sinisalo.

Walking up Stay Home Hill at night is treacherous, she added. And women who have to get home at night from Podunk College are stuck finding alternative ways because city buses have stopped running for the day.

Another woman brought up an incident where a woman was being assaulted on Brevard Boulevard and no one stopped to help.

That apathy toward women in danger seemed to follow the protest route around downtown Podunk last night.

"No one stops to ask what we are doing on the street anymore," said Sinisalo.

And she doesn't think it is a reaction to being aware and supportive.

She thinks people have grown uninterested in the issue and are unsure what they should do about it anyway.

Hopefully, some of that will be resolved next month when a violence against women symposium is presented.

Called "Freedom From Violence, A Basic Human Right," the symposium will examine what individuals and communities can do.

"People need to know what they can do as people, individuals and families," said Sinisalo.

The symposium will also take a historic view of the issue of violence against women, assess how far it has come and where people involved in the issue need to go.

Meanwhile, the municipal government announced today that the Community Development Fund has granted $12,250 to the Podunk Status of Women Council toward funding the Nov. 13-14 symposium.

-30-

Here's a possible rewrite:

Karen Sinisalo was disappointed with last night's Take Back The Night rally — no one asked what more than 50 women and children were doing on the streets, marching, singing and chanting.

It wasn't a case of the public being aware and supportive, said Sinisalo, a co-ordinator of the Elizabeth Walmer Women's Centre.

It was more like apathy: People have lost interest in women's fear for their safety and don't know what they should do about it anyway, she said today.

She hopes that will change next month when a women's symposium, called Freedom From Violence, A Basic Human Right, will examine how individuals and communities can help.

"People need to know what they can do as. . . individuals and families," said Sinisalo.

The city today announced a $12,250 grant to the Podunk Status of Women Council to help pay for the symposium, Nov. 13-14.

Last night's march, an annual event since 1992, ended with an open discussion at the United Church.

One speaker complained that when a woman was being assaulted on Brevard Blvd. no one stopped to help.

Sinisalo said bush trails used for jogging, bike riding or walking are never safe for women and walking up Stay Home Hill at night is treacherous. She said women have to find alternative ways to get home at night from Podunk College because city buses have stopped running.

Last night's rally was "about our freedom from violence. That is our basic right," said Sinisalo.

-30-

If you were paying close attention, you would have noticed there are facts missing from this story. What streets did the marchers use? Where will the symposium be held? Is a little more than 50 marchers a large number for Podunk? How many were there in previous marches? You might think of more questions.

Worth noting here is the kind of decision you'll often need to make. When I first tried the lead in this last story I wanted to say that Sinisalo was unhappy because the women and children weren't accosted. The first dictionaries I checked were old enough so that the first or only meaning of accost was to approach someone and to speak first. But more recent dictionaries said the word meant to approach aggressively, possibly with sexual intent. That idea had to be scrapped.

It's also worth noting that a sharper lead would have said that the 50 women and children were unhappy that no one asked what they were doing. But the original story didn't say that. It said that only Sinisalo was unhappy. The others probably were too — but you should not assume.

Did I mention that you should never assume?

Now it's your turn.

The following published stories (names have been changed) need to be rewritten. Do so.

PARKING

A preliminary report on downtown parking, prepared for the Chamber of Commerce, has been released. In June, a total of 73 businesses responded to a 21-question survey conducted by the Resource Centre. The results were reviewed at an executive meeting of the Chamber last week.

"The Town asked for our input on parking and traffic on Dunville Avenue," said Chamber President Alicia Ogalammi. "We felt this was a good first step, between the Town and the business community, to gather input rather than making arbitrary decisions.

"Prior to the survey we had a few members tell us they would definitely like to see better enforcement of parking by-laws, to assure customer parking in the downtown area.

"The most important finding in the survey was that most businesses felt a warning should be issued for parking offenses and, if parking in front of other businesses continued, tickets should be issued.

"Some businesses admitted to parking in front of their own, or their neighbor's business, or allowed their employees to park in those areas."

Fifty-eight of the businesses surveyed said they supply off-street parking while 15 do not. For some of the businesses, the town parking lot is an option however, 17 businesses felt the town should supply more public parking space.

"The Town should encourage any and all traffic in support of businesses," reads the report. Others, however, felt there was no need for a parking by-law.

If another parking lot were to be provided by the Town, a slim majority (35) felt the lot should be paid for by general taxation.

A need to ensure customer parking.

Slightly fewer respondents (30), thought a new parking lot should be user-pay and several more were unsure. One observer, however, said a new lot was not required, since the existing Town Lot was never full.

"We've also had members say that they definitely would like to see additional signage for the posted speed along Dunville Avenue. It's too fast for the two blocks between O'Connor and Niagara Street where people are angle parking," said Ogalammi.

The preliminary report was reviewed at a weekend Retreat for the new Town Council. A full report will be issued to the Town at a later date.

Ogalammi said the cost of the report is estimated at $900 with the Chamber and Economic Development sharing costs.
-30-

HEALTH

The Podunk Health Centre is set to receive a new general surgeon thanks to cooperation between the Regional Health Authority and Wing Squadron 15.

Maj. Allen Redwing, a military surgeon currently on deployment in Nigeria, will be returning to Canada in April.

After taking a couple of weeks holiday, Redwing will make the move from his current posting with the Bigbopper Garrison to CFB Podunk.

Wing Administration Officer Lt.-Col. Donald Clutterough says the military has been arranging to bring a surgeon to Podunk since Dr. S. Miller left the area in 1997.

"We have been working at it for quite some time," he said.

Clutterough added the military have very few surgeons in uniform and most of them are posted to major centres such as Bigbopper.

"It is in our best interest to post him here," he said. "The expertise Maj. Redwing will bring will be excellent for the area."

He explained the need for a surgeon in Podunk and Redwing's desire to be posted to Wing Squadron 15 combined to convince the military to arrange the posting.

Before beginning his tour in Nigeria three months ago, Redwing had been coming to Podunk about once every three weeks to perform surgeries as required.

Clutterough said Redwing grew to like Podunk on his trips to the area.

Wing Squadron 15 Dr. R.O. Listrone said a light caseload added to Redwing's desire to come to Podunk.

She explained in Bigbopper, Redwing did not have the amount of work needed to keep his skill level up.

With so many civilian surgeons in the city, he dealt only with military referrals.

In Podunk, Listrone said Redwing will be setting up a clinic at the health centre to handle both military and civilian patients.

When asked if military personnel would receive priority over the general public, Listrone said the time demands on a surgeon in Podunk would not require any priorities to be set other than taking emergencies first.

"I don't perceive it's going to be a problem," she said.

-30-

Interviewing

If, for instance, they have heard something from the postman, they attribute it to "a semi-official statement"; if they have fallen into conversation with a stranger at a bar, they can conscientiously describe him as "a source that has hitherto proved unimpeachable." It is only when the journalist is reporting a whim of his own, and one to which he attaches minor importance, that he defines it as the opinion of "well-informed circles."

British novelist Evelyn Waugh.

Dumb question: How do you like being 100 years old?
Bad answer (for the reporter): Fine.

Dumb question: How do you like being 100 years old?
Good answer (for the reporter): I wish I was 97 again and could still chase men.[*]

So who told you journalism would make sense? This is about dealing with people, not science.

However, there are methods (if not scientific, as least as close as you'll get in journalism) that can help with an interview.

The most important is to do research. Go to the newspaper's library (which used to be called the morgue, and maybe still is in some places) or start searching with your computer to find out as much as you can about the interviewee in the time you have. If you have lots of time, call friends, enemies, colleagues, etc. You may even have to read books.

Prepare questions. Use your imagination by anticipating answers that might be interesting. Run the five Ws through your mind.

Once you are face to face, take time to put the interviewee at ease especially if the person you are interviewing is not used to the press, or if it looks like a difficult interview. It will give you time to plan an approach to suit that individual. When you get to your first question, it helps to show that you know something about the subject.

Try to frame most of your questions so they cannot be answered with a

---

[*]See the subjunctive in the chapter on grammar.

Not chasing
men any more.

simple yes or no: What's the difference being 100 and 95? Can you still chase men? or women? (Your research might help here.) What do you do when you catch 'em? But you will still want to ask the dumb questions, for example, to what do you credit your longevity? and even how do you like being 100?

Organize the questions in advance in an order that could resemble the direction the conversation will take (but don't expect that to hold up), keeping in mind that you may run out of time and will want the most important questions answered first. Make sure you get the basic questions answered.

Now here's what may seem to be an obvious rule: Don't antagonize the interviewee. There are two major ways that happens.

1. The reporter pretends he understands a complicated subject. That makes the interviewee fear the dumb reporter will get it all wrong.
2. The reporter spends most of the interview expounding. Listen to the interviewee.

Some other points:

Try not to think only about your next question. Most of the time you want to be in control of the interview, but pay attention to what's being said so you don't miss taking the right direction and if necessary change to a different story. Interrupt as little as possible. You can come back to fill in the blanks if you have time.

If you haven't got as good an answer as you expected, try the silence trick. Don't say anything for a few seconds. Often the interviewee will react by giving more information, sometimes exactly what you are looking for.

Try to get exact answers — not "recently" but the date. Not "most of" but a figure. Get specifics.

In a complicated story, reconstruct the chronology with the interviewee.

Ensure early that what is being said is not off the record. If the interviewee wants to speak only on that condition, you must decide immediately whether to proceed or not. It's sometimes possible to change the interviewee's mind later when he or she has some confidence in you, but if you have agreed and there is no change, don't break the confidence. If your interviewee is used to the press and the conversation is on record, be reluctant to accept an off-the-record request after the comment. With the experienced, especially on a topic of public interest, everything should be considered fair game. But if the interviewee has never dealt with the press before, be fair. You know the consequences; make them clear and be understanding.

Pay attention to surroundings, to any extraneous events and to the physical aspects of the interviewee for any colour you may need for the story.

You may ask leading questions. You're not in a courtroom, but be aware that you may get a distortion. Make sure that you avoid that.

Be aware that the interviewee is approaching the topic from a different viewpoint than you. He or she may not know what a good story is. It may be up to you to dig it out.

Be suspicious. Look for evasions and lies. Learn about body language. You can sometimes catch someone out by asking a question for which you already know the answer. Even if you're not worrying about lies, ask that question to get the interviewee's own wording, and sometimes an unexpected answer that leads to a better story.

Be tenacious; don't accept evasions readily. Try the same question later from a different angle.

Don't be afraid to ask difficult questions. The interviewee is probably expecting them. But save them until you have established a rapport.

Learn to ask questions that help tread water so you can think for a few seconds. For example: "Let me check that. You said . . . . Is that right?"

Be curious about everything, right to the end. The interview isn't over until the interviewee is out of sight and hearing.

If for some reason it would be wrong to take notes during the interview, write them as soon as possible afterwards. Record the date and all other relevant information, like where the interview was held and who else was present.

Dress appropriately and give off the right signals; don't look bored by it all.

Ask if there is something else that needs to be in the story. Even with years of training, you will never be able to think of everything. Ask if there is someone else you could speak to for added information. Seek corroborating information whenever you have the need.

It's helpful to use a tape recorder, not only to ensure accuracy but also to unburden your mind so there's less distraction from writing down what's being said. But take some notes too and try using a stopwatch or tape counter to pinpoint important comments. That could save hours of transcription time.

Interviewing on the phone involves a different approach. Wasting time on small talk to try to put the interviewee at ease can be annoying. Get to the point quickly.

How you deal with the interviewee otherwise is a matter of your personality, how you understand human nature and your sensitivity. But there are three more major points to be made.

1. Look for The Twinge.

   The Twinge is a little inside voice that says, "Hey, wait a minute. There may be something here." When you get it, you'll recognize it. But it may be so vague that the natural tendency will be to shrug it off. Don't. It means you've probably hit on what will make the difference between an ordinary story and an outstanding one. You must make a conscious effort to follow through.

2. Look for an angle during the interview.

   It's not uncommon for reporters to come back to the office and spend hours searching for the point of the story. If you've been lucky enough to get The Twinge, you won't have that problem. If you see what you want during the interview it may also save you from calling back to get new information to fill out the angle. It may also let you start planning your story before you get to your computer.

3. Look for where you can go wrong.

After you've written a story about a complicated subject check back with the interviewee to make sure you haven't made a dumb mistake. You don't want to read the whole story back, but take the approach that you are too stupid to understand the technical stuff. Neither of you wants incorrect information published.

The Real Stuff

Reading someone else's newspaper is like sleeping with someone else's wife. Nothing seems to be precisely in the right place, and when you find what you are looking for, it is not clear how to respond to it.

British author Malcolm Bradbury.

Let's try some real stuff.

1. Break the class into groups of two and interview each other to write an obituary. Try to make the death suit your partner's personality. That might force you to get a good angle. After you've written the story, discuss it with your partner. Did you miss something? Did you get it all right?
2 Interview a fellow student on campus who has been there for at least two years. Get two stories from the same person: Why is he happy here? Why is he unhappy here? The object of the exercise is obvious.
3. Interview your instructor, all of you together, as a press conference. The topic: How does your class rate with others? Object of the exercise: To recognize when the subject is squirming, and how to handle it. Discuss the results with your instructor, after you've written the stories.
4. Choose a famous living person and write his or her obituary. If the person lives in the same town, you might have fun calling friends (obviously telling them this is an exercise only).
5. Invite VIPs (separately) to class for press conferences. Have them discuss their work in relation to the press. Try to find a story, then write it.
6. Select one of your classmates to be a mock VIP for a specific topic. Hold a press conference to look for a story. Write the story. Discuss the project afterwards with the mock VIP, getting comments about how the student felt he or she was treated.

So What *Is* News?

News may be true, but it is not truth, and reporters and officials seldom see it the same way.... In the old days, the reporters or couriers of bad news were often put to the gallows; now they are given the Pulitzer Prize, but the conflict goes on.

James Reston, former New York
Times journalist.

Now that you've learned how to write a hard news story, let's go back to something more basic.

What makes a news story? What is news?

The two best answers I've heard:

"Whatever I say it is." (Many editors)

"What is on a society's mind." (Mitchell Stephens, 1988, *A History of News*, New York: Viking)

The first answer is the result of the exasperation journalists feel trying to pin down an exact definition. They usually never think about it, they recognize news immediately.

The second answer is vague, but try to come up with a better one. Something similar is attributed by Melvin Mencher, in his well-read textbook *News Reporting and Writing* (Wm.C. Brown, Dubuque, Iowa), to Charles A. Dana, who ran the New York Sun during much of the last half of the 19th century: News is "anything that interests a large part of the community and has never been brought to its attention before".

There are some fun definitions too:

William Randolph Hearst (1863-1951) said, "News is something which someone wants suppressed. All the rest is advertising." Lord Northcliffe (1865-1922) of England was credited with defining news as, "What somebody somewhere wants to suppress. All the rest is advertising."

Philip L. Graham, publisher of the Washington Post 1946-63, said, "News is the first rough draft of history."

Those are views of news from on high. There are guidelines that help in day-by-day decisions, although by the time you get into the business, you won't be thinking about guidelines. You'll know, or you'll be working in a hardware store.

Impact is important.   *U.S. National Oceanic & Atmospheric Administration*

This is what you'll know:

The key concern, whether you think it consciously or not, will be **impact**. All the attributes that follow have impact on the reader.

For example, **importance**: There's more impact in 10 people being killed in an explosion than in 10 people arguing over lunch hour timetables at a home and school meeting.

But if its your home and school, and your child that's affected, which means you are affected, then the meeting may have more impact on you than the explosion. That makes **proximity** important.

Numbers and **size** are important: 20 people killed is a bigger story than 10 people killed. But that is weakened by proximity. If 10 people die in an explosion on your street, it has more impact than 20 people who die in an explosion in the U.S. and 300 people in a disaster on the other side of the world.

Now suppose you're working in a small town and one of the 10 people at that home and school meeting is the mayor, or a movie star who lives there. **Names** make news.

If this happened in a neighbouring town, the famous star would probably turn the meeting into a story, but the mayor probably wouldn't. Bigger names make bigger news and proximity as an attribute lasts longer in that case.

But news must also be **timely**. There's more impact in today's 10-car fatal pile-up on Main St. in Podunk than in yesterday's explosion because that is already old news.

Conflict is an important attribute. If a new law about school lunch hours passes quietly, it won't have the impact created by a good fight over the timetable.

The **unusual** or **bizarre** will also add impact.

And then there is **human interest**. To start with: sex, children and animals. You can't go wrong. **Crime** is a catchy topic too.

There is more to human interest, of course. Bring a new tax story down to a personal level, how it will affect you and your neighbours, and you've added human interest. You do the same in a workers' strike story by showing how weeks of low strike pay affects a large family. If you can add sex, children or animals to those stories, they will have more impact.

All that sounds confusing, doesn't it?

It isn't when you're in the middle of it, working on stories. It all makes sense then.

The Changing Of News

*Frankly, despite my horror of the press, I'd love to rise from the
grave every ten years or so and go buy a few newspapers.*
Spanish filmmaker Luis Brunel.

The descriptions of what makes news outlined in the last chapter were
accepted in the media for most of the 20th century. Before that English-lan-
guage newspapers had different interests and "news" had a different meaning. So let's have a little history lesson.

Those old papers were intended to be read by the elite, who were interested in politics and the movements of money, but not social or economic
reform.

That role was changed by the penny press, first started in North America
in the 1830s, and by yellow journalism, started in the 1880s by publishers
like Joseph Pulitzer and William Randolph Hearst.

Papers before the 1830s sold, by subscription, for five or six cents and
were long columns of type, usually verbatim and seemingly endless reports
of political debate, suitable for reading only by people with lots of leisure
time. The papers were opinionated and usually allied to political parties.

The New York Sun in 1833 was the first to sell on the street for a penny
and was shortly followed by the New York Herald, the New York Tribune
and the New York Times. They started to run police and local news and
human interest stories and circulation rose quickly from the usual few hun-
dred a day to several thousand.

In the 1880s Pulitzer and Hearst began making their pages sparkle with
graphic innovations and short stories with the kind of leads we use today.
They also tried to outdo each other creating sensational stories and were
soon selling hundreds of thousands of papers a day. If you use circulation
as a criterion, Pulitzer was the clear winner. But both were responsible for
the sobriquet "yellow press" although Pulitzer can claim the first step.

In 1895 Pulitzer's New York Sunday World ran the first newspaper
comic strip, Hogan's Alley, by Richard Outcault. One of his characters was

The Yellow Kid –
forerunner of yellow
journalism.

Courtesy of the Richard D. Olson Collection

a young boy in a nightshirt. The World's printers were experimenting with the first use of colour and ran the nightshirt in yellow. "The Yellow Kid" in Hogan's Alley became popular. Outcault switched to Hearst's New York Journal the next year and drew a new strip called Yellow Kid, using the same colour. Pulitzer and Hearst were the best known distributors of sensationalism in newspapers so the term yellow journalism soon came into common use.

But the yellow press was also involved in campaigning for social and economic improvements. Together with the rest of the penny press, during the great age of muckraking, they helped change the role of newspapers.

As these papers started attracting more advertising there was also a shift away from partisanship. Publishers found their biases were turning away too many readers and since advertising rates were becoming dependent on circulation, the new rule became factual presentation only. Readers could make up their own minds. Opinion was confined to editorials and by-lined columns.

A similar process occurred in Canada. Here the heroes were William Lyon Mackenzie and Joseph Howe, for us more political figures than journalists.

The meaning of "news" is still changing.

After World War II opinion-free news started to be questioned. Critics complained that the system accepted what sources said at face value, failed to put events in proper perspective or give sufficient background. The kind of disaster that could be created was brought forcefully before the U.S. public by Edward R. Murrow in his ground-breaking 1954 TV documentary on U.S. Senator Joseph McCarthy's communist witch hunt. At the same time journalists accepted the belief that it was impossible for a reporter to be totally objective.

How to solve the problem of combining social responsibility with impartiality is an on-going debate that has led the press through Watergate and Vietnam, the emergence of alternative papers like the Georgia Straight and the Village Voice, writers like Tom Wolfe and Hunter S. Thompson and broadcast shows like As It Happens and 60 Minutes. Trying to accept social responsibility and reacting to the changes created by television are thrusting reporters into roles for which few are prepared, such as leaders of public opinion and influential partners in setting political agendas.

Here's one opinion about the result, from Georgie Anne Geyer, a U.S. reporter and author writing in the Los Angeles Times on Feb. 4, 1979: "It was when 'reporters' became 'journalists' and when 'objectivity' gave way to 'searching for the truth' that an aura of distrust and fear arose around the New Journalist."

Here's another, from Jeffrey Simpson, writing in the Globe and Mail, May 2, 1988: ". . . it pains me to see the glibness and superficiality, the rushed judgements, and worst of all, this developing cynicism, which at heart is nothing more than a refusal to accept the admission of ignorance and the need to rectify it."

The next wrenching change to newspapers is coming from marketing. Competition from new media has lead to the disappearance of many independent small papers and to the growth of huge chains. The chains, their individual papers and the few independent papers remaining are turning to providing more service to advertisers. The obvious danger is to the fearless presentation of news and to the amount of space available for hard news and comment. The power of the advertiser may be enhanced with the growing convergence of newspaper, television and Internet staff under one owner.

Writing Well

Journalists do not live by words alone, although sometimes they have to eat them.

Former U.S. presidential candidate
Adlai E. Stevenson.

The first step in writing well is the same as the first step in doing anything well: You must understand fully what you are trying to do. For a reporter, that means understanding what your story is about, including its limitations.

That helps with the next step, getting the right angle for the right lead.

If you can do those two things well, plus get all the right information, the battle is half over and you are a valuable member of the staff, even if you will never be able to write anything better than your name. A good copy editor or rewrite person can work wonders.

But if you write well too. . .

Write in a straight line:

That rule is an example of the quirks developed by editors who spend years working with young reporters. The editors start to recognize common writing problems, then they develop rules to lay down to solve them. The straight line is one of my quirks. Your editors will have their own. More important: There are excellent books on how to write well that you should study. Everyone's favourite is probably *The Elements of Style*, by Strunk and White (William Strunk Jr. and E.B. White).

This chapter contains some of the most common problems I've seen.

The longest lasting writing fault of young reporters is a failure to make their ideas flow naturally from each other. That happens because reporters are struggling with how to get the facts down in proper order (sometimes in just any order), not with what's happening in the reader's mind. If you put into his or her mind certain thoughts at the end of a paragraph, you must begin the next paragraph with associated thoughts, or you disturb the reader. You can even write a long sentence, of almost any length, if you do not throw in clauses that make the reader jump around from one disconnected idea to another but instead have your ideas flow smoothly, in other words in a straight line, just as I have tried to do in this sentence, which I have now stretched out as long as I can without throwing you off course.

Here's an example of a convoluted structure. This is a real story as it appeared. Only the names have been changed.

> Justice Herbert Balcon today announced that he was recusing himself from the appeal hearing of Frank Rush.
>
> On Monday, April 12, legal counsel for Frank Rush, attorneys Allan Redwing and Stanley Ogba, had formally requested to the Court that Justice Balcon recuse himself from the appeal hearing on the grounds of ruling out any possibility of bias.
>
> This request arose from the fact that it was Justice Balcon who had made a ruling in a bail hearing for Frank Rush (at the time he refused to grant Rush bail) late last year, while he was on remand pending the outcome of his extradition hearing before Magistrate Lawrence Vaina. The Chief Magistrate has since ruled that Rush can be extradited, but the decision was appealed and the case will now be heard before a Justice of the Supreme Court.
>
> Justice Balcon, while giving his decision, stated that he would be submitting the reasons in writing at some later date.
>
> -30-

The problem starts right after the first paragraph, which is about what Balcon had done. The second paragraph starts with a date and two other people, the attorneys, and then winds slowly back to Balcon. That's hard to follow. There's no straight line.

Here's one way to KISS this story:

> Justice Herbert Balcon announced today that he's removing himself from Frank Rush's appeal against extradition.
>
> He was asked to do so last month by Rush's lawyers to avoid any possibility of bias.
>
> Justice Balcon had been involved with the Rush case late last year when he refused to grant bail while Rush was in remand waiting for the outcome of his extradition hearing.
>
> The Chief Magistrate ruled then that Rush could be extradited, but Rush appealed.

His appeal will now be heard by a Justice of the Supreme Court — but not Justice Balcon, who said today he'd give his reasons in writing later.

-30-

In many newspapers, especially dailies, that might have been rewritten by a copy editor, sometimes unbeknownst to the reporter. Copy editors, always under pressure, may also, in your opinion, butcher your story and leave you to figure out why. That is often hard to do without help. (Sometimes even other copy editors can't figure it out!)

Unfortunately, young writers are often left on their own on too many newspapers. There isn't time to turn you into the next Hemingway. That can't be done anyway by a copy editor or writing coach, but a good one can make a big difference.

Most copy editors, once they're happy with your lead, will look to see that all the information is there and that it's in a reasonable sequence. They will eliminate unnecessary words, check the spelling, maybe move a few paragraphs around and try to save you and the paper from a libel suit, then go on to the next story or headline.

Good editors, if they have the time and inclination, will explain, maybe from their own quirky viewpoint, why the changes were made. They will talk about more than writing techniques. There will arise such problems as fairness and logic, because you can't "write" journalism in isolation from the facts. You will find those discussions stimulating, especially if you're not afraid to argue a point, and your editor lets you. Good editors will be open to you changing their minds. If you find someone like that, take advantage.

More old quirks of mine:

• Don't repeat ideas:
That's the second most common fault (already mentioned in previous chapters) and the second hardest to eliminate. To repeat, it is easier to avoid repetition if you start off in the right direction with the right angle.

• Beware of the what-is:
What is is what happens when you write a sentence like this one.
Here's another: What is important is that you don't write a sentence like this.

64

"What is. . . is that. . . " (in the second example) should be a red flag. Even "what is" (also turned around in the first example into "is what") should be enough of a warning.

You should be saying, "What-is happens when you write a sentence like this" and "It is important that you don't write a sentence like this." If you get rid of those what-ises you will strengthen your sentences.

The same often, but not always, holds true for "that is" or "is that":

"The advantage of the new system is that it is more efficient. The disadvantage is that it leads to a loss of jobs."

"The new system is more efficient but it leads to a loss of jobs."

Most copy editors don't see the what-is or that-is problem because those sentences are a natural way of speaking, a form that does not usually work well in print. Some reporters will disagree; they say they do best when they write the way they speak. In most cases that's a cop-out for a news story. You may be a fascinating conversationalist, but when you speak to someone one-on-one, or to a group, you are using more than words to keep their attention. Just your presence is an attention-holder (even, for a while, if you're a bore).

Most write-as-you-speak stories are repetitious. They offer few ideas. Put them beside a write-write story and you'll see the difference, unless the reporter has purposely written in a speaking style. That takes work. Written dialogue is usually not the way real people speak.

The previous warning does not apply to your choice of words. Keep them simple and KISS the story.

- Quotes are great, but. . . :
  If you can say it better, do so, especially in the lead, unless you need the quote for the sake of having a quote, which usually is not a good excuse.

- Quotes are great, but. . . :
  Allenson said he would not attend the second meeting in the town hall because it was going to be stacked with ringers.
  "I won't go because the meeting will be stacked with ringers," he said.

Don't leave the reader dangling. *NASA*

You see that often. The writer and the copy editor are both too lazy to avoid the repetition.

> Allenson said he would not attend the second meeting in the
> town hall because "it will be stacked with ringers".

• Beware of dangling the reader:

If your lead says there are five reasons why some proposed law was rejected, or that someone had six complaints about an adversary, don't leave the reader waiting for later in the story. Explain right away what the five or six things are or make it clear they're coming up soon.

• Don't find different ways to say "said":

If you're searching too often for words like exclaimed, explained, indicated, outlined, etc., to replace the word "said" you've probably written awkward sentences. Rewrite.

• Writing is more than facts:

There are times when you need extra words to create a feeling or set a scene. Those can also be "ideas".

- Use the dictionary or your spell checker:

Most people think they can spell well. Many can't. Some don't even know which words are the difficult ones. Don't make your editors angry by making them do what you should have done. Look up the meaning of words too.

- Listen to the sound of your sentences (if you have time):

Your paragraphs and sentences should have a cadence that you hear in your head as you read them to yourself (not necessarily out loud). There should be almost a musical flow from sentence to sentence and from one part of a sentence to another. The same can happen with groups of words. For example, near the top of this chapter I wrote, "More old quirks of mine." I could have written, in the usual newspaper style, "Here are some of my quirks." "More old quirks of mine" has a ring partly because it recalls "that old gang of mine" and partly because the words work well together (which is why "that old gang of mine" is so catchy). "Some of my quirks" clunks. (Except in that last sentence; what a wonder words are! There's a kick in suddenly hitting on a phrase that works that well).

Some hints all editors agree are useful:

- Take a break:

Have a coffee, walk around the office, read a magazine, phone home, anything to do something else and forget about the story, especially a complicated one, if you have time. You will mull the facts around in your brain subconsciously and often what you are looking for will pop into your head unexpectedly.

- Be an old grouch:

If you have time, don't be satisfied the first time around, or the second or third. Reread to see what you need to rewrite. The best ideas often come after you've done the first or fourth draft.

- Use show and tell:

Use colour to show readers what you're talking about.

Instead of saying that someone was angry, tell how that person's face turned red, he swivelled in his chair and threw papers around, shouting. In some stories the atmosphere, the way someone looks or dresses, some minor details can be important.

Use anecdotes and action to make points.

- Organize:
If you have a long story, plotting it on paper can help.

- Eschew obfuscation:
That was a funny sign around in the 1970s. Few people took the advice seriously. Jargon, pomposity and euphemisms are much more common these days.

- Be active:
Try to avoid saying that a report from the Podunk police asking for more officers has been published. "Has been published" is a passive form. It's better to say Podunk police published a report asking for more officers. That's the active form, and stronger. It's even stronger to say simply Podunk police are asking for more officers. That puts your sentence into the present tense and you can talk about a report later. But don't avoid the passive voice at all costs. Sometimes it fits better than the active voice.

- The angle, the angle, the angle:
It's important in good writing because it can turn a boring collection of facts into ideas that grab the reader by creating an interesting point of view.

Here's an example of how that can work, an example that also illustrates how it can be hard to find the right angle. It comes from a book, *Yesterday's News, Why Canada's Daily Newspapers are Failing Us,* by John Miller (Fernwood Publishing, Halifax, 1998).

Miller, a professor of journalism at Ryerson University in Toronto and previously deputy managing editor at the *Toronto Star*, volunteered to work for free at a small town weekly during a sabbatical. He used that experience to contrast a small-town paper's connection with the community to what he sees as a big-city daily's disdain for its community. (It's a book worth reading.)

When he attended a local meeting at which farm union leaders complained about a series of roadside fines they said discriminated against farmers, he said he could have written a lead about how they planned to lobby politicians in Quebec to change provisions of the Highway Safety Act. That would have been the usual news lead. Instead, he said, he decided to capture the meaning of the meeting instead of the news.

His story described how government officials who didn't understand safety regulations and farm equipment turned the audience against them and admitted they couldn't explain the regulation they enforced.

"The story stuck a universal theme: a well-informed citizenry *can* stand up to bureaucracy and make it look foolish," he wrote.

He got the angle right, although he thought he was breaking one of the rules. The angle is the most interesting thing to your readers, a concept that includes importance. In this case it's obvious how it sets you off on the right foot and creates an interesting point of view.

• Throw all these rules away:

Not really. However, writing isn't rules. It's imagination and thought put into a form the reader can use, easily. You can break all the rules if you can put yourself into the reader's mind.

Writing Features

Newspapers are unable, seemingly, to discriminate between a bicycle accident and the collapse of civilization.
George Bernard Shaw.

There is one "secret" and two hard things to do when writing a long feature.

- The secret is the same as for a hard news story: get the right angle, but with a slightly different approach. In a long feature you need a narrow focus.
- Sticking to it is one of the hard things.
- The other has been brought up more than once: Do not repeat ideas. That's even harder in a long feature.

A long feature is usually a background piece, a profile, an investigation, etc., that is considered soft news, meaning generally that it does not have to run today.

But it is not a long discussion of Everything You Ever Wanted To Know About The Subject. It is also not Everything You Found Out About The Subject. That produces a turgid story.

That's why you need a narrow focus. Its purpose is to grab the reader's mind and drag it along a straight line, in effect to simplify the structure of your story: It sets a narrow goal and aims straight for it. And like anything that turns out to be simple, it's hard to do, harder than the two hard things mentioned above.

It's also hard to give specific instructions because each story is so different. Instead, here's an example of what happens. This is an excerpt from a critique for a former student:

Nice lead, but afterwards the story is disjointed. You don't have enough focus. It isn't enough to decide you want to describe what a singles bar is all about. You have to choose some aspect to concentrate on, or some theme to run through the story. As you've written it, you can't make up your mind whether you want to talk about the business end of it or what the atmosphere is like or what kind of people come there, etc. I think you wanted to talk about the business end and use that as a basis for telling what kind of people go there and what goes on. In that case, you have to organize the story in that way.

You can use the same first paragraph. Then you could describe how those two people compare in looks to the others, or what happens to them after that night. If you do the first, then you could say they're the kind of people who go to singles bars, then why, then how (the singles bar) has cashed in. If you do the second, then you could say that means they don't go to singles bars any more after they get married, but there are lots of new young people coming along who look at the bars as a good mate hunting ground, so (the singles bar) is cashing in.

Either way you've organized the story so the ideas flow in a straight line towards your goal, the full explanation of your theme.

To write a long feature in a newspaper, your theme, or narrow focus, should be based on something new for the reader.

That may seem a strange thing to say, but many inexperienced reporters want to write about events of world-shaking importance like the devastation of the Brazilian forests or the failing court system.

You can do so, but what do you have that's new? Will you repeat everything that has appeared in newspapers? That would produce that book no one can find room to print, or the 10-part series that would take an experienced team to prepare.

Look for the news angle.

Is there someone in your city or town who has just returned from Brazil with new information? Is some local company just starting to plan work in the Brazilian forests?

Are several local families complaining that their lives have been adversely affected by court delays, even though there have been promises of speeding up court proceedings? Is a local lawyer trying to convince the law society to change how it disciplines its members?

There is also room in a newspaper for summing up a series of events that

Is someone planning work in Brazil?   *Megavision Multimidia Ltda.*

have been presented piecemeal. Finding a news angle improves the story.

Once you have narrowed your focus, partly by deciding what you have enough information for, you must choose a lead that sets you off in the right direction.

While writing the story, you may be tempted to use a lot of information that doesn't fit the narrow focus because it is interesting or exciting, or maybe just because you have so much of it. There could be 10 or 20 times more than you need. You have two choices: Be ruthless in rejecting it all because you have the right focus, or change the focus so the new information fits. Sometimes you'll find you have chosen the wrong focus, but most of the time you should KISS the other stuff a fond farewell.

Now comes the second hard thing to do: not repeating ideas. That fault usually occurs in features that wander all over. Sometimes the fault is the focus. Sometimes it's the writer. If you find yourself repeating an idea, you've done something wrong. Rewrite.

There are lots of examples of wandering features, but making you read one here is cruel punishment for someone who hasn't done anything wrong. Instead, pick a couple of topics and dig in. If you want to start with stories that are almost guaranteed to give you trouble, choose a local artist and a help-line telephone service.

One warning about a fault that I've seen too often: There's a tendency to take a slow approach into a feature, sometimes by presenting the common-place at too-great length so the writer can follow with a punchy contrast. That can be boring, especially when it's about a person. Turn the sequence around. If you make the reader curious about the person first, even normally boring details can become interesting.

Remember the reader's mind: He or she doesn't know yet everything you know. What may be fascinating to you may be meaningless to the reader.

Writing For Broadcast

I am a journalist and, under the modern journalist's code of
Olympian objectivity (and total purity of motive), I am absolved of
responsibility. We journalists don't have to step on roaches. All we
have to do is turn on the kitchen light and watch the critters scurry.
                                    U.S. journalist P.J. O'Rourke.

KISS EM.

That's the biggest hurdle you may have to overcome if you go into broadcasting after being trained in newspapers or in academe. Keep It Simple,
Stupid — Even More. The writing, that is.

You must remember this: A KISS is not a KISS on radio or TV if you
write some sentences that work well in newspapers. Medium-length ones
are too long. Most of your sentences should be short, punchy and constructed as subject-verb-object.

Here's how to do that: Think about the form your sentences take when
you speak. After all, someone has to speak what you are writing.

For example, here's a simple sentence from the middle of a newspaper
story (a real one, with some facts changed):

> Wood Lathe Turners Local 2238, which represents 1067 Podunk
> workers, voted Sunday afternoon at Baylor High School after a
> speech by the provincial president, Alan Krtanjek.

Read it out loud and you'll see how it could be a little hard for a listener
to follow.

You would probably say something like:

> The wood lathe turners union voted Sunday after hearing a
> speech by their provincial president, Alan Krtanjek (Ker-tan-
> jeek). The union local represents about one thousand Podunk
> Workers.

The biggest
hurdle.

Francesco Hayez

Read that out loud and see the difference.

You probably noticed more than a change in structure.

Most important: There are facts left out. You probably agree the most important ones are still there. That's done partly because broadcast stories are short — they're measured in seconds. A couple of minutes is a long story. You must be even more selective, or more to the point, than in a newspaper.

Spell numbers out in words so it's easier for the newsreader.

Use round figures where you can to make the point because exact figures are harder to grasp.

If the name has a rare pronunciation or a difficult one, spell it out for the newsreader.

Here's another newspaper sentence, a real lead that appeared in print, with some facts changed:

A dispute between this city's symphony orchestra and its fired star is headed for the courts today after the violinist emerged from a meeting with his former employers yesterday to announce he plans to file a lawsuit and a human-rights complaint.

It's a little complicated, but works in a newspaper. Try reading it out loud.

Now try this:

The former star of Podunk's symphony orchestra says he will sue and file a human-rights complaint because he was fired.

Bernard Fiddle, the violinist, announced his plans today after meeting yesterday with his former employers.

(That's a better lead for a newspaper too, not only because it's easier to understand, but also because it avoids repeating the idea of a dispute, contained in that word, in the words "heading to court" and in "file a lawsuit and a human-rights complaint".)

More rules:

Use the active voice and present tense whenever possible, but not if that creates awkward wording. Instead of using the passive voice in a sentence like, "A vote to strike was taken today," you want to use the active voice and say, "The workers voted to strike today." To put that into the present tense, you want to say, "Workers are ready to strike. They voted today to…"

Don't write with contractions, like "can't" and "didn't," which can sound like "can" and "did". Let the newsreader make those changes.

Give the attribution, the "who-said-it," before the comment: "Police said the victim was a known criminal," not "The victim was a known criminal, said police." The first example is a simpler construction, therefore easier for the listener to follow.

Use action verbs a lot.

But don't use lots of numbers or names. They can be numbing.

Besides sentence structure, there is one other major difference between newspapers and broadcasting.

Broadcast stories use a lot of audio and video clips. The broadcast writer, especially in TV, weaves words around them. That creates a different approach to a story than in a newspaper.

In a newspaper all your ideas must be expressed in words. In TV, choosing the video pictures comes first. You write what you don't have on tape. And you don't always have to describe a scene.

Now go back to some stories you've already written well and turn them into broadcast stories.

Writing For The Internet

I still believe that if your aim is to change the world, journalism is a more immediate short-term weapon.

British playwright Tom Stoppard.

The "nut graph" is colourful newswriting jargon.

It's the paragraph where you give the nut of the story, where you tell the reader why he's reading it, especially in a news feature if you don't have a lead with the five Ws.

These days in newspapers you sometimes find the nut graph anywhere from the first to the 10th or 20th paragraph. Those will often be long paragraphs too. That's a lot of reading before finding out what the story's about. Not every reader will stay with a story that long in a newspaper.

The same holds true for a computer screen. (It's a good thing you're reading this in a book, or you would probably never have gotten this far.)

Internet researchers have found that most readers of news stories won't go past the first screen if you don't grab them with the nut graph. That harkens back to the old newspaper days when an editor would rewrite any story that didn't have the nut in the first two or three short paragraphs. But the Internet is where you go for unlimited amounts of information. How do you handle what seem to be two opposites?

I'm glad I asked, because it's time to get that nut graph in here.

You cope by putting the nut graph in the first screen. You can then build a complicated story with what newspapers call sidebars, another bit of jargon. A sidebar is a secondary story that runs beside the main one. On the Internet it's a link.

Here's an example of how that might work. In a previous chapter, about how the treatment of news developed, you can find this paragraph:

A similar process occurred in Canada. Here the heroes were William Lyon Mackenzie and Joseph Howe, for us more political figures than journalists."

The following is the content within the image, representing a web browser window displaying "Town Crier Online":

Town Crier Online - Your source for local Toronto news and community information.

http://www.towncrieronline.ca/main/main.php?direction=viewstory&storyid=4366 — Google

MyEbay GREAT ATL...E COMPANY Apple .Mac Amazon eBay Yahoo! News

Town Crier 25
ONLINE.CA
1979–2004

Pick your Edition | Locate a Business | Search our Sit GO
Make us your Homepage | Town Crier Main Page Tuesday, February 1, 2005

News	Local News
Opinion/Editorial	Canadian Headlines
Arts & Entertainment	Search Archives
Sports	
Food & Fashion	
Home & Garden	
Kids & Families	
Classifieds	
Business Directory	
TC Event Planner	
About Us	

in memoria...

Local Caribbean street scene inspired TV movie and play

(Posted Date: Monday, January 10, 2005)

By Sandie Benitah

The Caribbean community on Eglinton Ave. West was the backdrop of an hour-long TV drama late last month and will also be the focus of a new play in the Mirvish Theatres.

Although the Vision TV production chose an area just outside our own community to film the movie — the Lansdowne Ave. and Dupont St. area — the set was designed to emulate our own local street culture.

The show Da Kink in My Hair centres around Novelette's, a fictional beauty salon on the Eglinton strip that is a popular meeting place for the community. Both the television show and the play follow the same plot — the story of a Jamaican mother Novelette and the hardships she experiences running a successful business while being a single mother. The story also touches on the lives and experiences of her female clients.

Sheryl Lee Ralph portrays Novelette, who people may remember from her roles in Designing Women and Moesha. It was directed by Tonya Lee Williams, star of the daytime soap opera The Young and the Restless.

Vision TV held a drama competition that awarded three prizes of $100,000 to independent producers to encourage them to make movies that reflect the city's cultural diversity. Da Kink in My Hair was one of the winners.

LOCAL CHARACTERS: Playing hangers-out in an Eglinton Ave. beauty salon in the play Da Kink in My Hair are (front) Sheryl Lee Ralph as Novelette, Trey Anthony as Joy, and (back) Ngozi Paul as Starr

TC Business Directory
Find a local business fast!

TC Features
TC Member Services
Recommend-a-Site
Advanced Search
Tell-a-Friend
Contests

TC Online Poll
Experts say cigarettes are losing their appeal. Do you think most teens agree?
○ Yes, I notice fewer kids smoking in public.
○ Yes, the kids I know say it's no longer cool to smoke.
○ No, nothing's changed except they're hiding it from adults better.
○ No, if anything more teens are smoking these days.
VOTE RESULTS
This poll was

Community Resources

TC Event Calendar
Submit an Event
<< Feb. 2005 >>
S M T W T F S
1 2 3 4 5
6 7 8 9 10 11 12
13 14 15 16 17 18 19
20 21 22 23 24 25 26
27 28

Grab 'em on the first screen.

Courtesy of Multicom Media Services

I didn't write anything about Mackenzie or Howe, but if you knew little about them your interest would probably be piqued. In a newspaper there might have been sidebars written, although they might not have been used because of lack of space. In broadcast there's little chance there'd be any further reference. In a book you'd find a bibliography. On the Internet those two names would be linked to stories about them or to sites with more information – and more links that lead to even more links.

It's interesting that this newest form of communication, which is revolutionizing our society, is in some ways returning newswriting to its Middle Ages. It's not only the nut graph that's finding its way back to the top of a story. The inverted pyramid, out of fashion these days in print, is back in favour in short news stories.

Otherwise, writing a newstory for the Internet is the same as for a newspaper. But the work could be a lot different.

There have been predictions that the Internet reporter will one day have to write the stories, take pictures and videos and get it all onto the Internet, updating all along. We all know people with two left hands who are great at what they do, as long as it's not something technical. Now there's an e-version of a one-armed wallpaper hanger.

Taking Pictures

We need not be theologians to see that we have shifted responsibility
for making the world interesting from God to the newspaperman.
U.S. historian Daniel J. Boorstin.

If you are not a trained news photographer but your paper needs a two-way reporter, you can probably use some simple hints for posed pictures.

None of these will turn you into a great photographer if it isn't in you, but they can make a difference.

We'll start with the good old angle, this time in a physical sense.

Instead of shooting straight ahead, try taking the picture from a slight angle. Don't make it extreme unless you want a strange effect (usually not a good idea). What you're after is impact, which in a photograph can come from a simple and slight change from the usual.

For example, when taking a head and shoulders, many photographers will seat the subject at a slight angle and have him turn his head towards the camera. Don't try to shoot from above or below unless you want a weird picture.

You could use the KISS principle too. Don't get too much into the picture. If you're illustrating a story about a cabinet maker, show one or two items and get the subject's face close to them. You may not need the rest of his body, unless there's something about it you should show, like huge hands; normally feet don't add much. If you need the hands, have the subject holding something close to his face.

A simple thing like putting on an unusual hat or catching a facial expression or having someone kiss a giant mask can "make" a picture. Don't just plunk things and people side by side and click.

If you're going to KISS a picture properly, you must also be aware of the background. It's simple enough to move a subject away from busy wallpaper or from a vast space that will turn out black to about a foot away from a clean, light wall or something else simple. (If it's a head and shoulders and you're using a flash that comes away from the camera, raise it high and

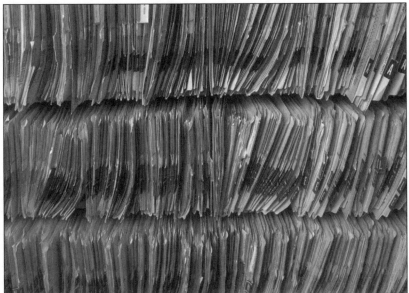

Patterns make pictures.

point it down at an angle so the shadow on the wall is reduced. Don't raise it so high that you add shadows to the face.)

If you're taking a picture outdoors in strong sunlight you can use the flash to get rid of the shadows on a face. If you have no flash, move the subject into shade.

If the background is important, get the subject close to the camera. (This takes for granted that you've learned how to use the equipment and understand depth of field.) You usually don't need all the background. You need to illustrate what it's like and have a person as the main focus.

It also helps to get that person doing something, anything simple that matches what you are illustrating. For example, if you are showing a yacht club, you can have the subject in the foreground tying something to the deck while you stand at an angle that shows background. Make the action suitable and natural.

If you're shooting more than one person, move them close together, especially their heads if all you want is faces. If there are a lot of them, try to use what's at hand in an imaginative way. For example, can you line them up a staircase? If they are studying building plans can you frame them in a pleasing way around the sheets of plans? Don't be caught having more people in the picture than you want. If they insist, take the picture, but make sure you get what you want too.

If you need a handshaking picture get the subjects as close as possible. That eliminates a lot of background, which usually adds nothing to the photo. And it fills the picture in the paper with the important images.

You should fill your viewfinder with those images before taking the picture. That means getting close to the subject and eliminating feet and even hands if all you want is a face. In that picture of the cabinet maker you may not need all of the two items you've chosen; take only half of each and you've come in closer to the face. Changing the angle can sometimes fill a viewfinder. The bigger the image the more impact.

If it's not just someone's face you want, look for patterns, for example, the snaking of fire hoses shot from above, road signs that line up, books piled on a desk, people in relationship to objects. Photographers love brick walls, for good reason. Try to visualize what things will look like when the photo is printed. And don't always get the person up front. Look for the striking image.

If you're at a news event, don't just take the fire hoses. Get a shot of the whole scene then zero in on the smaller details.

In some shots you can try what is called letting the reader complete the action: shoot the medal an instant before it is pinned or the cap placed.

Even if you are not a great photographer, use your imagination.

Finally, if you're not into digital photography yet, film is cheaper than sending someone back to reshoot. If you try lots of different ideas and come back with lots of pictures, you may hit it lucky with one of them. Of course, you avoid that problem with digital cameras. They let you know immediately if you got that perfect shot.

What Makes A Good Reporter?

When I joined the paper in 1923 they said it was steady work.
Journalist Ted Reeve, when the Toronto
Telegram folded in 1971.

My daughter chose, on her own without encouragement, to become a reporter. She went through wanting to be a lawyer, a psychiatrist and a writer, pretty good sensibilities to bring to journalism. But what she found she loved most once she started working was being sent out to deal with people and things and the world. That's a great combination, even if the opinion comes from a father.

She also has what Andrew M. Osler, who was a professor at the University of Western Ontario's School of Journalism, described as the characteristics of good reporters when he was writing *News, the Evolution of Journalism in Canada*:

> Few modern journalists will admit to it, but most half believe that there is something very special about them, something in their genes. Call it talent or an innate sense of what is newsworthy — it is a quality that sets news people apart. In reality, a good sense of language, a lively curiosity, the ability to observe intelligently, and perhaps a touch of P.T. Barnum's sense of showmanship, are journalism's special skills.

My daughter would probably have no trouble admitting that she thinks there's something very special about her. She also has the other qualities, including a good sense of language, which these days, unfortunately, has little to do with grammar or spelling. (She also has a good sense of humour and won't object to that statement.)

What do you bring? Will you be a good reporter?

All those I've known have these qualities: They read a lot and know a lot about the world around them, which they find fascinating. They are

They think they're special and they like people.   *Gulf High School, New Port Rickey, Florida*

observant, understand human nature and are sympathetic. They like people. But they are skeptical about many things they are told and can often see through cover-ups or fudging. Sometimes that comes from feelings and hunches. If they see a wrong they want it righted and will be tenacious and imaginative in their efforts.

Those are the qualities you start with. Now you must learn the job.

The most important part is simple:

Make contacts, as many as you can. Keep track of them in a file. Keep in touch with them. Most of your good stories will come from people who tell you things. The more you talk to people the more people will tell you. That becomes especially important if you are on a beat. But even as a general assignment reporter you will find your list of contacts invaluable.

That's it. If you recognize a story when it hits you in the face, you are probably a good reporter. (You'll make a better reporter when you recognize a story that doesn't hit you in the face.)

Sound simple?

If you have most of the qualities above, it is. A friend used to say being a reporter was much easier than working for a living.

That doesn't mean you won't have to put in long hours on the telephone or searching the Internet or reading reports and dreary books or knocking on doors or having what may seem like endless interviews to find a simple fact. There will be some drudgery involved and some frustrations, but mostly you'll enjoy the work.

Will you also enjoy asking a mother for a picture of the son that was killed that day? No, you won't, especially the first time, but it will not be as hard as you think. Will you have fun getting jostled in a scrum or being crowded while taking pictures? You'll have to answer that one yourself.

Libel

If I'd written all the truth I knew for the past ten years, about 600 people — including me — would be rotting in prison cells from Rio to Seattle today. Absolute truth is a very rare and dangerous commodity in the context of professional journalism.

U.S. journalist Hunter S. Thompson.

There's an old joke (predating today's non-stop TV news and the Internet) that goes a long way to explain how Canadian law relates to journalism:

In the court system in France, where the Napoleonic Code is used, you are guilty until proven innocent.

In Canada you are innocent until proven guilty in court.

In the U.S. you are innocent until the papers come out in the morning.

If you are ever involved with a libel case in Canada you probably won't think that joke funny.

Libel laws here are meant to bend over backwards to protect members of the public from the publication of any falsehood that would do them harm. As an added attraction for journalists, those charged with libel aren't equal before the law to other citizens facing charges: Those charged with libel must prove in court they are innocent instead of having someone else prove they are guilty.

Other laws that affect the press are contempt of court laws, meant to ensure the accused gets a fair trail.

Let's look quickly at libel first.

Libel is a printed statement, photo or drawing that imputes immorality, the commission of a crime or dishonourable conduct that exposes a person to hatred, ridicule or contempt and leads to a loss of income. Slander is the verbal form of libel.

Note that I did not repeat that what you print has to be untrue to be a libel. Truth is a perfect defence, but you must prove what was written was true.

The need to prove truth has saved a lot of dishonorable people from exposure. It has also stopped the publication of a lot of harmful gossip and hearsay.

The next most important point: It does not matter if you printed the libel by mistake. If you can't prove what you wrote to be true, you have libelled someone in law. Printing a retraction may help in many ways, but it won't get you off the hook if the injured person won't accept it.

That means you must be precise. Here's an example of what could happen:

You are told by a police officer that a charge will be laid against a person that afternoon. You write that the charge has been laid. But at the last minute no charge is laid. Your paper publishes the wrong information. Whoops! Wait for the phone call. It is no defence to say you were reporting what the officer told you. It also doesn't help if you say the officer said police were planning to lay charges. You have damaged the person's reputation (unless, of course, that person has had dozens of similar charges laid previously).

As you have probably noticed, there are some scurrilous, untrue and unfair comments about people that get published. There seldom seems to be a story about an editor or publisher going to jail because of them.

What is fair to print?

Meetings of the House of Commons and provincial legislatures are privileged, therefore anything said there can be repeated, even fuddle duddle. But you must be fair (give the other guy his rebuttal) and accurate.

Other lawful meetings of any kind to which the public is invited have what is called qualified privilege. If you are accurate and fair you can print whatever is said, and let the guy who said it be damned, but try to get the other side into the story.

Official written statements from organizations in which the public has an interest, as long as those statements are meant for the public, have qualified privilege.

If a libellous statement is made at a private interview, you print it at your own and others' risk. The reporter, the printer, even the distributor can be liable in a libel case.

Fair comment on public issues gives writers the widest possible latitude. You may say some outrageous things, as long as you do not impugn another person's character and as long as it's possible for other people to hold the same wild, even prejudiced views.

Almost anything said at a trial is privileged. The exceptions are any comments about an accused's record or confession made at a preliminary hearing or inquest, which are trials, or made anywhere else, at any time close to the final trial. If they are brought up at the final trial itself, they may be reported. The intent is to try to prevent a jury from hearing anything except the details of the case itself.

But that offence would not be libel, because the report would be true. It would be contempt of court. You would be jeopardizing a fair trial.

Contempt laws try to prevent newspapers from influencing a jury. If the trial is by a judge only, you could probably print anything true and not be in trouble because judges are considered too knowledgeable to be influenced by the press. You are also free to report details of a case if you do so shortly after information is laid for a trial that may be months or years away. If the case is to be tried in Vancouver and there's little interest about it elsewhere you can say what you like in Ottawa or Halifax.

You are also free to criticize the way a judge handled a case, as long as it is not a personal attack, and is fair. Courts, in our democratic system, are open to criticism. But if you want to discuss the merits of a case after a judgement, you must wait to make sure no appeal is made. If it is, you may not comment. You might be influencing another jury.

This outline of the law and the press is so brief that you must not rely on this information for your sole guidance. I have tried to give you an idea of how the law looks at the press, not rules to follow. Ask your editor if you have the slightest doubt. In fact, consider doing so even if you have no doubt. Libel laws are complicated and frightening. They frighten editors and publishers too. That's why many news organizations have lawyers at hand to help make decisions.

Ethics

What a squalid and irresponsible little profession it is. . . . Nothing prepares you for how bad Fleet Street really is until it craps on you from a great height.

British politician Ken Livingstone.

"He pitched good."

There, in a nutshell, is the kind of dilemma you face making decisions involving newspaper ethics.

Every baseball fan has read that comment from managers many times. If you were writing before the 1980s you might have corrected the grammar, especially if you were quoting someone in government or business. Reporters then were instructed that most people don't speak as correctly as they write and would probably want the change made. But today you hear the manager saying "He pitched good" on TV and radio, and a good reporter is also supposed to tell it like it is. But if you keep printing bad grammar are you feeding the growing ignorance about the proper use of English? Is that part of the dumbing of the population? Does the press have a responsibility to the language?

How would you decide? How would the others in your class decide?

Discussions of newspaper ethics, like this one, all deal with the public's right to know. Everyone has a right to know that most baseball players and managers (like other people) don't speak English properly, that many take drugs, get into fights in bars and cheat on their wives and are not great role models for young people. But as this case shows, there is often in journalism no one answer to a problem that satisfies everyone. That's why this chapter is full of questions.

The questions ask how far a newspaper should go for the information the public should have. There are more serious questions than whether you should correct someone's grammar. For example, is breaking the law justified sometimes? If you think so, are you willing to accept the same consequences that would affect other members of the public? How much of a normal life should a reporter have to forego?

Does he pitch good or well?   *IMSI*

Consider this:

A reporter covers up his role to sit in an improperly closed meeting at which public issues that should be aired openly are discussed. It's easy to answer that the reporter is justified in hiding his identity.

But what gives the reporter that right when journalists criticize a police officer or secret service agent who pretends to be a reporter? How far is the moral jump to an undercover police officer (or a reporter) enticing someone to break the law? Why shouldn't anyone have the right to lie or do whatever a reporter considers justified, if a reporter can get away with it?

Could such deception in the long run be instructing society that you can get what you want by lying? Will the reporter's honesty be questioned by his contacts in the future and hinder his newsgathering?

Suppose the reporter is under cover at a meeting of a political party and some delegates, including elected politicians, make newsworthy comments about strategy that they would never repeat if they knew reporters were present. Suppose they talk about some serious defect of a political leader that no one else knows. Would you publish the information and the name of the source? Would you be doing harm to the career of that source, someone who did nothing wrong? If that career is ruined, how serious would it be to that person and how many other people would be harmed? On the other hand, is it the kind of information that could save other people from harm? Is there another way to get the same information?

Sometimes reporters will use illegal and unethical methods to get stories they can't get otherwise. They are saying, "Trust me." As a member of the public, how far would you trust a journalist who is not a member of a governing body that has powers of discipline? Press councils, still in a formative stage, have no real power, certainly not with cheap tabloids.

It was only about a generation ago that many reporters believed it was most important to get the story any way possible.

There are situations in which the value of dissimulating clearly outweighs the harm of the offence, for example, when reporters, both visible minorities and "accepted" races, ask about buying the same house to investigate the reaction of real estate agents or vendors. Or reporters may create a problem in a car that can be easily repaired to see how many garages try to cheat them. Reporters are, in those cases, no different from any member of the public and they should be treated as such, not differently as they would be in closed meetings.

But a reporter in such cases is asking for special privilege to be permitted, in effect, to lie. (A lie can be something meant to deceive or give a wrong impression.) Even in the car example the reporter created a wrong impression, pretending that he or she didn't know what was wrong.

Special privilege carries with it special requirements. Do journalists today meet sufficient requirements?

What would the requirements be?

There are some general rules that journalists now consider valuable, but they are not fully developed.

For example, some media outlets have rules that reporters should refrain from joining political parties or any kind of public movement, from accepting freelance jobs from companies other than newspapers, from having business relationships with news sources, and from accepting gifts of any kind, even small ones. Journalists, these outlets say, should have no conflicts of interest and the public should know there is no outside influence. Is that realistic? Can a reporter be nothing but an observer in life? Most reporters aren't built that way. They make friends and friends in the news can have influence. They have strong beliefs. They want to invest to protect their old age. If a reporter's personal and business life is to be restricted, should the same rules apply to publishers and owners? The possibility of undue influence on the news is stronger in their case than with reporters because a newspaper is also a business and depends on advertising. That is a vested interest. Is it fair to ask reporters to do what newspapers, publishers and owners cannot do?

An example: In recent years economic pressures led some publishers to relax rules that prevented travel writers from accepting free trips. Now these stories sometimes tell the reader who paid for the trip. The public knows, but is the coverage honest? Will the public know if it isn't?

How would you enforce the rules?

Would public censure be enough? Who would bring the facts to the public and could that happen whenever necessary?

A professional organization with power could enforce rules, but those who believe in a free press strongly oppose any form of licensing, which a professional organization would have to do. If you want a free press you must leave it open to anyone, including the gutter press that sometimes forces responsible papers to jump onto stories they would prefer not to run. And if there is a professional organization with power, who would watch the watchdog?

Here are two examples, one Canadian the other American, to illustrate ethical problems in journalism and how they were handled.

In 1989 Global TV's Ottawa bureau chief Doug Small was one of a group offered a copy of the leaked 1989-90 federal budget. The person who first leaked the information breached a confidentiality agreement. Small accepted and broadcast the information, breaking an embargo, before the budget speech, something never done before. The reasoning: To show the government had bungled and to prevent a select few from taking advantage of the information before the rest of the public had it.

In 1978 the Chicago Sun Times, deciding it could not get the information any other way, had reporters and photographers pose as bartenders and waiters and operate a bar to prove that inspectors and police officers were soliciting bribes. The series won many awards, but not the Pulitzer Prize because the reporting methods were considered unethical.

Other ethical issues that arise, like plagiarism, the theft of pictures and the choice of biased words are, I think, more general ethical problems than particular to newspapers.

A Reporter's Role In Society

Journalism could be described as turning one's enemy into money.
British journalist Craig Brown.

Many of us older newspapermen (there weren't any "people" in those days) can remember what reporting was like in the middle of the 20th century. Those of us who were young male reporters in Ontario got our journalism education bending elbows (nobody just drank) with the guys in beer parlours. That's what they were called, and women ("society page sob sisters") were not allowed into our room.

The most fascinating topics of conversation were the latest tricks pulled to get the story and what was wrong with the paper you worked for. The beer tasted better (at 10 cents a draft) with lots of salt to keep the bubbles going, and with a couple of pickled eggs you didn't need supper. I don't imagine the women wanted to be in the same room. They had their own called Ladies and Escorts. Being an escort was the only way we could get into that other room. None of us cared — it wasn't any nicer.

If someone had started to talk about the "pseudo-environment" of Walter Lippman or Harold Innis' *The Bias of Communication*, or the responsibility of the media in "the emergence of a new civilization" that it was creating, he would soon have been sitting at an empty table.

Our only pressing responsibility was buying our round.

It's true that everyone's attention was caught by Marshall McLuhan's "the medium is the message". No one understood it, but it was fun.

Since those days newspaperpeople (what a funny word) have generally become responsible journalists concerned about their roles in society and what harm or good they might do. That probably has a lot to do with the development of journalism schools, the wide acceptance of other disciplines into journalism, a growing demand for accountability and the increasing cost of beer. These days newspapers expect some academic knowledge when they hire. In the old days the only qualification you needed to become a reporter was to be able to ask for the job.

A great many journalists now understand what the medium is the message means. They know all that other stuff too. You should all know all that other stuff. That's why I suggest you read the book from which I have summarized most of the rest of this chapter and which I have already mentioned, *News, The Evolution of Journalism in Canada*, by Andrew M. Osler.

In one chapter Osler runs a connecting line starting with Plato through U.S. journalist Lippman and French scholar Jacques Ellul to Canadians Innis, an economic historian, and McLuhan, a scholar of the media.

Osler finds that Plato and Lippman, and many philosophers over the centuries, had a coinciding view about perceptions of life.

Plato wrote about a cave where imaginary men chained all their lives to one spot assumed that wall shadows cast by firelight were reality everywhere in the world.

Lippman wrote early in the century about the need for humans to construct a simple model of our complex world, a pseudo-environment, so we could manage our lives. This pseudo-environment sends us stimuli to which we react and which dictate our behaviour in the real world. They also influence the way we think about things we have never seen or experienced.

Lippman, says Osler, took a step further than others by recognizing the dangerous potential in this "stereotyping".

How do all those stimuli from the not-quite real world alter, or do they alter, reality? How much of a role in this pseudo-environment does the mass media have?

In Lippman's time, when TV was in its infancy, the news media were not as powerful an influence as they are today. He thought their influence was modest.

Ellul, who lived through the days of the Nazi and Soviet Union's propaganda machines, considered the media played a dominant role. He extended the idea of a pseudo-environment into an expanded meaning of propaganda, used by states and society "to surround man by all possible routes, in the realm of feelings as well as ideas. . . . It furnishes him with a complete system for explaining the world, and provides immediate incentives for action." The individual on the receiving end, lacking strong family and religious community reference groups, and moved from the simple rural life to urban confusion, craves the propaganda.

Without the mass media, says Ellul, there could be no effective propaganda.

Osler writes: "A state monopoly, or a private monopoly is equally effective and he (Ellul) adds that the trend in the Western democracies to ever-increasing concentration in the private ownership of mass media creates a circumstance increasingly favourable to propaganda."

Ellul also developed a new concept for the word "technique" — it isn't just the machinery and the technology that gets things done, but also how they get done, all the means of doing it, all the human activity involved, which includes propaganda. Without propaganda there is no technique.

It is from here that Innis and McLuhan move on. They gave important expression, says Osler, to the "idea that media systems and their technologies might be especially consequential in humankind's society-forming relationship with technique".

McLuhan and Ellul, says Osler, meet "where they seem to have much in common . . . where the mass media, especially the technologies of the mass media, must be recognized as critically shaping the most fundamental circumstances of human existence."

McLuhan wrote that "media . . . are messages in the sense that they determine and embody what is to be considered appropriate social organization at any given time."

The next step was the famous statement: ". . . in operational and practical fact, the medium is the message."

Innis, to whom McLuhan said he owed great intellectual debt, wrote about the same topic:

"We can perhaps assume that the use of a medium of communication over a long period will to some extent determine the character of knowledge to be communicated and suggest that its pervasive influence will eventually create a civilization in which life and flexibility will become exceedingly difficult to maintain and that the advantages of a new medium will become such as to lead to the emergence of a new civilization."

That was published in 1951 in *The Bias of Communication*. Will the Internet fulfill his prophecy?

There's lots more good stuff in News.

Finally, here's a quote from German historian Oswald Spengler, on the same topic, published in 1926 in *The Decline of the West*:

The press today is an army with carefully organized weapons, the journalists its officers, the readers its soldiers. But, as in every army, the soldier obeys blindly, and the war aims and operating plans change without his knowledge. The reader neither knows nor is supposed to know the purposes for which he is used and the role he is to play. There is no more appalling caricature of freedom of thought. Formerly no one was allowed to think freely; now it is permitted, but no one is capable of it any more. Now people want to think only what they are supposed to want to think, and this they consider freedom.

Grammar

Doctors bury their mistakes. Lawyers hang them. But journalists put theirs on the front page.

Anonymous.

Chickens lay eggs, people don't.

Chickens lay eggs in public, people lay each other in private. But not always in the media.

No one knows how many people the media have accused of committing illegal acts on beaches and in other public places.

Maybe those media outlets haven't been sued because the grammatically incorrect public doesn't know better and the grammatically correct public is getting used to the increasingly common incorrect use of the different verbs to lay and to lie, and all the other mistakes that are appearing more and more frequently.

That is one place where newspapers are in the vanguard; they are usually the first in serious print media to get the grammar wrong.

The major fault isn't with the reporters. Most are young and schools ignored grammar for so many years it's no wonder some graduates can't put a sentence together properly or write correct English. Many think they "should of" had more grammar. They don't know the difference between an adverb and an adjective and so don't know that "He pitched good" is bad.

A reporter's mistakes should be caught at the desk. But for many years their work was handled by journalists with little experience who let too many mistakes get by, even in some of the country's major newspapers, and especially in sports pages.

Copy editors used to come mostly from the reporting ranks. They were older and knowledgeable about the language, but not always good handlers of writers and writing. Newspapers therefore made an effort to recruit people who were good at working with other people's stories. Some came straight out of journalism school.

A good knowledge of grammar can develop early, but understanding how language changes and then finding a balance between the two usually comes from a few years' experience working with words.

This doesn't mean that the good old days were faultless. In fact there used to be some stupid rules. You had to say an amount was $300 "more than" the allowance, not "over" the allowance, because "over" meant "physically on top of". Never mind what the dictionary said. You could not have someone evacuate an area (he or she had to be evacuated from) because the first meaning of the word would have had that person emptying his or her bowels. You could not start a sentence with "but" or "and". Whoever made that rule probably also considered the King James version of the Bible a masterpiece even though almost every second sentence begins with "and".

But at least those old guys (there were almost no women on desks) knew how to use words like "like" properly. You wouldn't catch 'em dead not knowing the difference between "fewer" and "less". They knew when to "imply" and not "infer". They knew the difference between "its" and "it's" and even tried to handle the most difficult of all, "which" and "that". How many people today know they all have different meanings and uses?

What's more, they tried not to split infinitives and they didn't do "alot".

And have you noticed that question marks are starting to disappear from newspapers (and other printed matter)? How many people have heard of parallel construction? Can you avoid a dangling modifier or incorrect syntax? Do most people even know what the subjunctive case means?

Do you care? If you want to write clearly, you should.

Here are some of the distinctions of the words and problems mentioned above.

To lay: That's a transitive verb, which means the subject of the sentence is performing an action on something or somebody. It takes an object. Today you lay a knife on the table. Last week you laid the knife on the table.

"Laid" is a part of the verb "to lay", the principal parts of which are "laid" and "laying".

"Laid" is not a part of the verb "to lie", which is an intransitive verb, which means it does not take an object.

So if you want to talk about placing yourself prone in bed, you can't use the word "laid". You need the verb "to lie" and its principal parts, which include "lay," lain" and "lying". Yes, it can be confusing.

These are the important distinctions: You can lie down for a nap after lunch (if you do it today), but not lay down for a nap (if you do it in the present tense, like right now). Well, you could lay yourself down, but why not just lie down? But you can say you lay down for a nap — yesterday, because "lay" is a past tense of the verb "to lie". You can lie in bed all night, or you could have lain in bed all night, but if you laid in bed all night you'd need a good night's sleep in the morning. Get a good grammar book to lie down with and we'll just lay the matter to rest at this point.

Should have: And would have if only grammar were taught properly. There is no such thing as "should of" or "would of".

Good: That's an adjective, which modifies a noun. Well is an adverb, which modifies a verb. Good pitch. Pitched well.

Like: Most newspapers have given up trying to preserve the difference between "like" and "as if". To keep it simple: The word "like" is a preposition that links two similar things or nouns: He looks like an athlete. She has a punch like a hammer blow. "As if" is a conjunction that links two clauses or sentences: She stopped running as if she had hit an invisible wall. He acts as if he were infallible. These days people would say he acts like he is infallible (which causes another strange problem — see the comments on the subjunctive).

Fewer: That word involves numbers, "less" does not. You can have 15 fewer things, but you can't have 15 less things. You can have less enthusiasm, but you can't have fewer enthusiasm. My wife, who had trouble with the difference, discovered this trick: If she thought she could use either "less" or "fewer" in a sentence, then "fewer" was the right word.

Infer: You infer from what I imply. Example: If I tell you that Joe Blow was arrested yesterday after a break-in and that a charge of break-and-enter had been laid against a male suspect, you may infer that Joe Blow was charged with break and enter. That's you coming to that conclusion. I may have implied that. The difference is in who's doing what. You, as the recipient of the information, may take a meaning from it, you may infer something. But all I can do, as the one giving the information, is imply a meaning to you. I can't infer a meaning to you. Only you can infer a meaning from what I say.

It's: It breaks the rule, it's the exception. The apostrophe elsewhere means possession. For example, "The man's hat." But in this case, its, without the apostrophe, means possession. So "it's" is the contraction. It means "it is," just as "here's" means "here is".

Which: Here's one that will drive you nuts. Or is it, Here's one, which will drive you nuts? Well, in this case I mean "that" but there is such a mind-numbing set of rules that even Fowler (*A Dictionary of Modern English Usage*, by H.W. Fowler, revised by Sir Ernest Gowers,) seems to throw up his hands. In the long section on *That* he writes, in the 1994 edition: "The relations between *that. . .* and *which* have come to us from our forefathers as an odd jumble, and plainly show that the language has not been neatly constructed by a master builder who could create each part to do the exact work required of it... The two kinds of relative clause, to one of which *that* and to the other of which *which* is appropriate, are the defining and the non-defining; and if writers would agree to regard *that* as the defining relative pronoun, and *which* as the non-defining, there would be much gain both in lucidity and in ease. Some there are who follow this principle now; but it would be idle to pretend that it is the practice either of most or of the best writers."

Therefore, to be defining, we need to say, "Here's one that will drive you nuts." I'm talking about a particular "one", a particular rule that will drive you nuts."

Strunk and White say "that" is the defining, or restrictive pronoun, "which" the nondefining or non restrictive. A restrictive clause defines the antecedent noun. A non restrictive clause adds information about something already identified, and is set off by commas.

The lawn mower that is broken is in the garage.
(That tells which lawn mower.)

The lawn mower, which is broken, is in the garage.
(That adds a fact about the only lawn mower in question.)

Now, is "That" correct in those two sentences in parentheses?

Split infinitives: Splitting infinitives is not a grammatical crime, as most newspaper writers used to think. But for a while they seemed to be reacting so strongly against what used to be a rule that they would rather produce a clunker than not split an infinitive. Here's an example, the start of a sentence by a regular columnist in one of the biggest papers in the country: "As junior man, part of my job was to every Friday wash down those black-and-yellow markers...." Part of his job every Friday was to wash down markers, not to split infinitives.
This writer made another goof. See the next rule.

Dangling modifiers: This is so common most people don't notice it. An example: After bending down to eat the hay, the man pulled the horse's head back by yanking hard on the reins. That sentence says the man bent down to eat the hay. The subject of the sentence is the man, so he must be doing the bending.
Here's a real example out of a newspaper, with the name changed, to show how easily the mistake can be made: "I guess I should first tell you that having tested these recipes, the author, Richard Writer was indeed preaching to the converted." The sentence says Mr. Writer tested the recipes. That's not what the writer wanted to say. That could have been written, "Having tested these recipes, I guess I should first tell you that the author, Richard Writer, was indeed preaching to the converted."
In the previous rule, the newspaper article said, "As junior man, part of my job was to...". Who or what was the junior man? It wasn't "part" or "job". The sentence could have said, "As junior man, I found part of my job was to...".

A lot: Not alot. All right? Yes, not alright. Anyone? Somebody? Yes. Awright!

Parallel construction: Its purpose is to make life easier for the reader. Here's an example of lack of parallel construction:
The board decided that in the next year it would
• add a wall to the centre,
• build a well,
• lower a ceiling,
• the treasurer successfully asked for a new bookkeeping system, and
• build stands for the basketball court.
Item 4 starts with a subject (the treasurer) while all the others start with verbs (add, build, lower and build). Item 4 should say, "buy a new book-keeping system for the treasurer", so the clause doesn't jerk the reader's mind around.

Syntax: That's the grammatical arrangement of words so that you say what you want to say and not produce something like a dangling modifier.

Subjunctive case: It's used mostly when what's said isn't fact, but a wish or possibility. For example, in the chapter on interviewing, that 100-year-old said, "I wish I was 95. . . . " That's grammatically wrong. She should have said, "I wish I were 95." And in the sentence earlier in this chapter, where "like" has replaced "as if," you should be saying (incorrectly), "These days people would say he acts like he were infallible," but that sounds terrible to me. It sounds fine if you say it like this (or as you would have in the old days): These days people would say he acts as if he were infallible.

I'm going to throw in here something that (which?) bugs me. Olympiad is not a synonym for the Olympic games, even though I've seen one dictionary that accepts it in a sports context. The Olympiad is the four-year period between the Olympic games. The first Olympiad came between the first and second Olympics, so you can't interchange the 2nd Olympics and the 2nd Olympiad or 40th Olympics and the 40th Olympiad.

And finally, Z: @#$^%$&%&*! In Canada, it's zed, not zee.

The Last Word

It was because of me. Rumors reached Inman that I had made a deal with Bob Dole whereby Dole would fill a paper sack full of doggie poo, set it on fire, put it on Inman's porch, ring the doorbell, and then we would hide in the bushes and giggle while Inman came to stamp out the fire. I am not proud of this. But this is what we do in journalism.

U.S. syndicated columnist Roger Simon.

Have fun.

-30-